VOICES INT

The High Price
I Had To Pay

SENTENCED TO 12 1/2 YEARS FOR VICTIMIZING LEHMAN BROTHERS BANK

WRITTEN BY:
JAMILA T. DAVIS

VOICES
INTERNATIONAL PUBLICATIONS

The High Price I Had To Pay: Sentenced to 12 1/2 Years For Victimizing Lehman Brothers

© 2015 by Jamila T. Davis

This book is a real-life story about the events that led to the imprisonment of author Jamila T. Davis. All names and events are true. The information in this book can be verified through public record. (See U.S. v. Davis Docket No. 2:05-CR-0482-JLL-01 (District Court of New Jersey) or Lehman Brothers Bank FSB v. Ellis et al., Docket No. ESX-C-103-03 (New Jersey Superior Court, Essex County))

Printed in the United States
Second Printing 2015

ISBN: 978-09855807-9-7

Voices International Publications
196-03 Linden Blvd.
St. Albans, NY 11412
"Changing Lives One Page At A Time."
www. vocseries.com

Typesetting by: Jana Rade www.impactstudioonline.com
Cover Design by: Keith Saunders www.mariondesigns.com

TABLE OF CONTENTS

FOREWORD

When I wrote "The High Price I Had To Pay" in 2013, I had no clue that my book would spiral the formation of a powerful prison reform movement. After sharing my book with inmates whom I was housed with at Danbury Federal Prison Camp, it was discovered that many of us, who were white collar offenders, experienced similar injustices within the U.S judicial system. Joining forces with these women, a study was conducted by Cultural QuantiX that revealed we received 300% greater sentences than male white collar offenders who committed the same or similar crimes. The number was a shocking 400% for African American females (see www.womenoverincarcerated.org). The results of this study led to the formation of WomenOverIncarcerated (WOI), a nonprofit organization of which I am a co-founder. WOI was created to shed light on the lengthy sentences incarcerated women face and its effect on society, to expose the injustices female offenders face within the U.S. judicial system and to provide resources and support to incarcerated women and female ex-offenders.

Within the last two years numerous organizations and even notable Congressional Representatives have taken note of our efforts, and the organization has been successful at bringing awareness to the epidemic of Over-Incarceration of women to the general public. It felt good to finally see people taking note of our struggles. This charged my passion to create viable change, which led to the creation of "The High Price I Had To Pay" book series. This series gives incarcerated women a platform to share their stories. Each volume features women serving decade plus sentences for non-violent crimes. Not only have our stories helped to create awareness about the epidemic of women in prison, our books are being used as educational tools to deter at-risk youth from crime. Most recently, Volume 2 of this series was awarded as Top Ten Book of The Year for at-risk youth and youth in custody by "In The Margins" Book Committee, featured in the School Library Journal (see www.slj.com/2015/02/awards/top-2015-titles-for-youth-in-custody-or-in-your-libraries/).

At the time I wrote this book, I was a nervous prisoner who thought this effort was my last shot at justice. I had no clue my courage would result in helping multitudes of people. This is a great achievement to me and reassures me that I need to continue to fight. Today I know there is purpose in my pain. I believe in my heart one day in my life time change in the U.S. judicial system will indeed come! Until then, I will continue to march on!

Jamila T. Davis

INTRODUCTION

"Is it fair that corporate giants get to blame 'small fries' like myself, whom they recruited but they walk away scott-free?"

My name is Jamila Takiyah Davis. I am an African American, 35 year old, single mother of two children. I was born and raised in Queens, New York.

On July 16, 2008, prior to the 2008 Financial Crisis, I was sentenced to 151 months in federal prison for bank fraud. I have served 5 years of that sentence. I was accused of being the 25 year old mastermind who victimized the now defunct Lehman Brothers Bank (Lehman) of 22 million dollars in mortgage loans through an elaborate scheme which the bank alleged that I created. These allegations were initially made by Lehman attorneys, who made a formal complaint against my colleagues and me to the New Jersey U.S. Attorney's Office in early 2003. The part that the bank's attorneys left out of the complaint was the fact that their own employees were the ones who structured the deals, instructed us what documents we needed to get each loan approved, and who further aggressively solicited more deals after the initial fraudulent loans were funded. Long before it was revealed that the corporate policies at Lehman were based on fraudulent lending practices, I tried to expose the "inside" fraudulent conduct that I witnessed first-hand in my case. I wondered how the government didn't recognize that novices in the industry, such as myself, didn't have the ability to structure fraudulent deals and get them approved without the help of insiders. Although I took responsibility for my part,

7

my checkered past hindered me, and my allegations of inside fraud were quickly dismissed. I was in no league to contend with my powerful opponent-Lehman. The bank's prestige and clean image made their credibility golden. At the time, no one believed that the bank would knowingly engage in fraud. Consequently, I became the notorious 25 year-old that developed a massive scheme to defraud Lehman.

Once Lehman attorneys successfully painted themselves as victims before the government, they were able to have the properties in question in my case, which were not in foreclosure, deeded over to the bank. In total they received 9 luxury estates in prime, upscale areas in New Jersey, valued at over 30 million dollars. Instead of accepting full price offers from buyers who were prescreened by the U.S. Attorney's Office, Lehman attorneys arranged a private sale to a vested investor in Lehman for an upwarded 14 million dollar discount! While Wall Street savvy elite got to enjoy the dividends created by the "sweetheart" sale, I was left to serve a 12 1/2 year sentence. My lengthy sentence was not based solely on my admitted participation in the scheme. There were two major factors that significantly increased my sentence: (1) I was labeled as a leader/organizer, and (2) I was left with a large exaggerated loss amount figure that Lehman itself created through the inside sale of the properties to one of its affiliates.

I was sentenced just 59 days shy of Lehman's collapse on September 15, 2008, which spiraled a world wide financial frenzy causing the 2008 Financial Crisis. Had I been sentenced after Lehman's demise, my fate might have been different. Lehman's bankruptcy findings revealed to the world that fraudulent lending practices were embedded in the corporate policies of the firm, and it showed that Lehman in fact orchestrated, encouraged and funded billions of dollars in fraudulent loans. This evidence confirmed my allegations that I did not mastermind the scheme that I admitted to having participated in. In fact, I was recruited by one of Lehman's affiliates and instructed step-by-step how to get each fraudulent transaction funded. Unfortunately, none of this new evidence was ever heard in my case.

Despite the revelation of the shocking intricate details of Lehman's fraudulent mortgage lending practices orchestrated by their high ranking officials, I am left to serve a very lengthy sentence while not one Lehman executive was punished. Is it fair that corporate giants get to blame "small fries" like myself, whom they recruited but they walk away scott-free? You be the judge.

It is my goal to detail the events that led to my incarceration and reveal the direct roles that Lehman affiliates and Lehman employees played in my case. I am first to admit: I am no saint and I should have never taken part in the fraudulent scheme. At the time, I justified my actions with my intent. The goal of the scheme was to fix up properties in high-end areas and sell them to my celebrity clients at a profit. I never intended to cause anyone a loss. I had no idea that my participation in this scheme would ruin my life. I learned the hard way the severity of the consequences of taking business short-cuts. My purpose of sharing my story is to expose the injustices in my case. I do not contend that I should not have been punished for my role in the scheme. My argument is that I was used as a sacrificial lamb by former Wall Street giant, Lehman, to cover up the bank's own wrongdoings. As a result, I was "over" punished and the real masterminds were allowed to escape. It is my prayer that my story will be heard by people who have the power to make a difference and that the scales of justice will finally be balanced.

This Is My Story!!!

CHAPTER ONE
Young, Savvy &
Ambitious

"My newfound prestige, and my desire to maintain it, clouded my judgments. I felt it was okay to take business short-cuts. In my mind, gaining the esteem of my peers outweighed any consequences I would suffer if I got caught."

I was born and raised in Jamaica, Queens- a working, middle-class section in New York City. In my area several of my friends who I grew up with entered into the hip-hop music industry. They became famous rappers and music executives. I noticed that these individuals had a desire to obtain credit to purchase cars and homes. Even though their financial status had significantly increased, they lacked the knowledge to obtain the credit resources they needed to buy certain assets.

With the needs of my peers as an incentive, in 1998 I became a real estate broker, establishing Jamila Davis Realty in Queens, New York. The same year, I also opened New Beginnings Financial Services in Brooklyn, New York. This company was created to assist clients to establish or restore their credit, and to help them obtain financing to purchase homes and cars. I started off my business helping clients obtain nontraditional financing at higher interest rates to establish their credit. My company quickly flourished. Through my business I became well acquainted with celebrities, music industry executives and professional sports figures who sought my services. My notoriety led me to become a lead financial go-to-person in the hip-hop music industry.

In my early twenties, I was a thriving business woman. I gained a position of trust with many of my clients. My newfound prestige, and my desire to maintain it, clouded my business judgments. I felt it was okay to take business short-cuts. In my mind, gaining the esteem of my peers outweighed any consequences I would suffer if I got caught. I rationalized my unethical dealings with the theory: no harm, no foul. Therefore, I linked with an outside source who had the ability to go in all three credit bureaus and illegally erase bad credit and add positive credit lines to my clients credit profiles. Adding this service to my business significantly increased my client base, which also expanded to the general public.

Consequently, in early 2000 I became a target of an investigation launched by the U.S. Marshall services, which led to my conviction of conspiracy to commit mail fraud. I pled guilty and was ordered to pay restitution and sentenced to 5 years probation. After my conviction, I discontinued my credit repair services and got more involved in real estate.

In 2001, I recognized an opportunity to buy, renovate and sell distressed properties at a significant profit, so I opened Diamond Star Financial Inc., a consulting and real estate firm, in Teaneck New Jersey. My real estate investing started on the low end. I bought multi-family distressed properties in low income areas and renovated them. After renovations, I sold these homes to my clients as income-producing investment properties.

Back in 1999, I was introduced to Alpine, New Jersey by Kareem "Biggs" Burke (Jay-Z's former business partner, who was part owner of Rockefeller Records). The houses in Alpine reminded me of castles that I used to see in story books which I read as a child. Most of the homes, also known as mansions or estates, were built on 2 acres or more of land. They had amenities such as outdoor and indoor pools, tennis courts, basket ball courts, bowling allies, movie theaters and saunas. As the clients that were introduced to me increased in financial status, more and more of them desired to live in this prestigious area that I was intrigued by.

In early 2002, I was approached by one of my clients Akinelye Adams, a popular rapper at the time, who was known for his provocative song, "Put It In Your Mouth." He was seeking to buy a home he had found in northern New Jersey, which he was going to use as a location to shoot an adult, cable reality show. He advised me that he needed a house that included enough bedrooms to accommodate the adult entertainers that would be featured on the show. He wanted my assistance in obtaining financing for what he perceived to be the perfect location. Adams introduced me to his realtor Debra Friedman, who was a well-known realtor in northern New Jersey. She had just closed on a 8 million dollar home in Saddle River, also a part of northern New Jersey, sold to hip-hop mogul Russell Simmons.

Adams desired to purchase a mansion in Cresskill, at 497 Piermont Rd. Cresskill is a small upscale neighborhood in northern New Jersey that borders Alpine. The house was originally listed at 1.7 million dollars and was owned by the Liguand's, a couple in the classical music industry who was in the middle of a divorce. The couple desired a quick sale, so they were willing to reduce the price of their home. I helped Adams with negotiations on the property, which Friedman facilitated. We were successful in getting the Liguand's to accept an offer of 1.1 million dollars. On behalf of Adams, I hired an appraiser, John Witty, to assess the property's true value. I was shocked when the appraisal revealed that the property was actually worth 2.2 million dollars, double the price Adams was in contract for! Excited about the potential return on the investment, Adams quickly decided to go into contract.

Before I could arrange the financing on Adams' deal, I got a call from Adams who stated that he needed a larger house for his production. He found an estate in Pomona, New York that better suited his needs. After speaking to Adams, and per his instructions, I called his realtor, Friedman, and canceled the deal. She and I thought it was a bad decision to lose out on the house in Cresskill which we knew had substantial equity. After speaking to Friedman, I decided I would try to purchase the house myself and utilize it as a real estate investment. I believed I could do some minor renovations on the home, including landscaping, and sell the house to one of my clients for a substantial profit. Therefore, I secured the property under contract in my own name.

Back in the spring of 2001, I was introduced to Nicholas Infantino, a mortgage broker at United Mortgage Services, by a realtor friend of mine, Shakir Saleem. I was told by Saleem that Infantino had just obtained the financing on a home for one of his clients, Rob Walker, a well-known music executive and a manger of the popular rap group, the Neptunes. Saleem advised me that Infantino understood the nontraditional financial needs of entertainers, considered as independent contractors, who didn't have regular income but periodically received large sums of money for their work. I met Infantino and referred him clients to test out his services. He successfully closed on a few of those deals, which included a luxury condominium for my client Ed Holmes, who at the time was the co-manager of platinum-selling rap star Nelly. Because of my positive experiences with Infantino's services, and his ability to creatively structure deals, I thought he would be the right contact to secure my own personal financing for the property on Piermont Rd. Therefore, I decided I would reach out to Infantino to see if he could help me.

CHAPTER TWO
.The Set Up!

" Infantino advised me that we were safe, because he had a contact inside the bank that would push the file through. Amazingly, like clock-work, the deal was magically approved."

In early 2002, I approached Infantino seeking his assistance to help me finance the Cresskill property in my own name. I told Infantino that I desired a loan that would be based on the appraised value of the house, leaving funds for renovation. He ran my credit score and said I would not qualify on my own. Infantino advised me that he had a bank that would approve the deal, but to obtain quick funding I needed a client with a 630 or higher credit score to hold the property in their name.

I proposed to one of my clients, rapper Freddy Foxx aka Thomas Goldson that he consider holding the property in his name as an investor, as Infantino suggested. I explained that we would fix the property up, sell it and mutually share in the profits. He agreed, and I gave his information to Infantino. Infantino ran Goldson's credit and gained a pre-approval from Lehman Brothers Bank FSB. The pre-approval was issued with a detailed breakdown of the income Goldson was required to make and the documents needed to close the deal. Infantino advised that Goldson's income had to be in access of $400,000 per year. He stated I needed two paystubs, two years tax returns and two months bank statements. I advised him that Goldson didn't have income that was in that range, Infantino stated it didn't matter as long as Goldson would

THE HIGH PRICE I HAD TO PAY

make the payments on time. He advised me that the phony income documents were an "ornament" for the file to pass inspection, so it could be sold on the market. I understood this to mean that the bank was okay with receiving "fake" documents.

I followed Infantino's instructions to the letter. I provided all the documentation that he requested, yet I was concerned that the amateurishly designed, fictitious income documents would not pass the bank's scrutiny. Infantino advised me that we were safe, because he had a contact inside the bank that would push the file through. Amazingly, like clock-work, the deal was magically approved.

In the beginning, I wasn't knowledgeable about how the deals were actually structured. I simply followed instructions. I quickly learned that Infantino was using the appraised value of the homes as the contract sales price on each deal. My partner, Shaheer Williams hooked Infantino up with a lawyer, Daniel Ellis who helped Infantino structure the deals in a format that allowed each closing to meet the bank's closing criteria. To my understanding, what we were doing was common practice in the mortgage industry. Both the mortgage banker and the lawyer had substantial experience with structuring similar deals.

After the first loan closed, Infantino aggressively solicited me for more deals. He said his inside contact in the bank had called him stating the bank was looking to close more jumbo loans. Not only did Infantino receive a large commission on the deal, so did his inside contact. Infantino suggested I arrange a meeting with him and my realtor Friedman. During this meeting he advised my partner, Williams, and myself, that if we bought up all the low-end houses on the market in this prestigious area, and renovated them, we would essentially increase the property value on all the houses in the area. Ultimately, it would also increase the return we would make when we sold the houses. Infantino's plan sounded good and he offered the financing, so we attempted to execute it.

While renovations were taking place on the first property, we found an estate that sat on the top of a hill in Alpine, that was directly next door to the owner's of Haagen Dazs' residence, on Cassandra Drive. With Infantino's help, we purchased this home through an estate sale for a discounted price. On this deal, I brought in my client Charles Stanton, who was the Vice President of Dr. Dre's Aftermath Records. As before, I followed Infantino's instructions and Stanton closed the deal in his name. The property was originally listed for 3 million dollars. We negotiated the purchase price down to 2.1 million dollars, but the property appraised at 4.4 million dollars, as-is-value, based on the comps on the market.

During the second transaction, I learned more details about the way the deals were being funded. One of Infantino's main contacts at Lehman was Diane Bauer. She was a lead underwriter at Aurora Loan Services Inc. (Aurora), located in Maryland, which was an affiliate company of Lehman. After the fact, I discovered that Lehman had set up Aurora in 1998 to be the company's sham mortgage arm. Through an inquiry I had initiated in 2011 to the Office of the Comptroller of Currency (OCC)(formerly the Office of Thrift and Supervision (OTS), I learned that Aurora was not authorized by the OTS to service or close loans on behalf of Lehman in 2002, the year the deals in my case closed. The OCC also stated that Aurora did not become an authorized service company with the OTS until 2003, and officially became a subsidiary in 2004. Despite that fact, in my case Aurora improperly acted on Lehman's behalf, originating, approving and servicing all seven loans in my case, without proper monitoring or supervision from the OTS, as required by federal banking law.

Bauer, underwriter at Aurora, would fax Infantino a list of conditions that needed to be met on each deal. In turn, Infantino would turn Bauer's list over to me, and I would provide the false documentation. At first, I wasn't sure of the depth of the involvement of the bank. It didn't become clear to me the exact role that the underwriter played until we attempted to get Goldson funded on a second multimillion dollar mortgage loan. Goldson closed on his first loan for the property in Cresskill, in April 2002. Approximately 6 months later, we attempted to get him approved to purchase a second property in Saddle River, valued at 4.4 million dollars. The larger purchase price required Goldson's income to be higher. As before, I got the paperwork for the deal that Bauer requested, yet I made a huge mistake!

Once the paperwork was submitted, Bauer suspended the loan file. She stated to Infantino that the paystubs and W2s conflicted from the first set that we had used to close the first loan. The first deal required that Goldson make approximately $400,000 a year. The second loan required that he make closer to $600,000 a year. I thought the gig was up and this error would prevent us from closing anymore deals. Exactly the opposite occurred! To my surprise, Bauer instructed Infantino how to clean up the file. She stated we would use the old documentation and get a letter from Goldson's accountant stating Goldson had an increase in income. She also instructed us to get a letter from a moving company and a rental contract for his current home. Once again, I followed the instructions and Goldson closed on a second, 3 million dollar plus, loan in a matter of weeks. With the help of Bauer, in less than a year Lehman had funded over 4 million dollars in mortgage loans to Goldson alone, despite the huge red flags and conflicting financial documents we sent to the bank! After the second loan closing for Goldson, I knew for sure the bank was directly tied into the fraudulent funding of our deals.

CHAPTER THREE
Lehman's Betrayal

"Then all of a sudden, instead of remaining Lehman's ally we became the bank's foe. Unknown to us at the time, we were turned in to the U.S. Attorney's office by Lehman attorneys who accused us of defrauding the bank. I was confused, I thought we were all in this together."

Within a span of a year, we closed on seven deals funded by Lehman, totaling approximately 22 million dollars, all underwritten by Bauer. Each closing was based on the inflated sales figures that matched the appraised value of the houses. At the closing of each home, we set up an escrow that included the amount needed to renovate each property and one year of mortgage payments. The goal of the scheme was to renovate each property within a year and sell them to wealthy clients. Then all of a sudden, instead of remaining Lehman's ally we became the bank's foe. Unknown to us at the time, we were turned in to the U.S. Attorney's office by Lehman attorneys who accused us of defrauding the bank. I was confused, I thought we were all in this together.

It was later discovered, in early 2003 an internal investigation at Lehman led them to go after the properties we had financed through their bank. At this time, not only were our properties in northern New Jersey sought by the bank's attorneys, so were a slew of properties in Beverly Hills, that were obtained through similar financing. These properties were purchased by Charles Fitzgerald and his colleagues, whom we never met. Coincidently, they utilized the same office of Aurora Loan Servicing Company in Maryland, who funded close to 80 million dollars worth of fraudulent mortgage loans for Fitzgerald and colleagues. Instead of eyebrows being raised about the similarities of our cases and how so many fraudulent loans were able to pass the bank's scrutiny, Lehman was taken at its word and became viewed as a victim. Essentially because it was their complaint, eyes were blinded to the inside fraud that actually took place, and the bank was off the hook. As in my case, Lehman attorneys fought and got back the high end properties in Beverly Hills. According to Fitzgerald's attorney, several of the properties were sold to Lehman attorneys and to insiders for huge discounts!

I first learned there was a problem with our financing through a fraud alert issued by FBI agent Sean McCarthy on 04/04/03. This alert was sent out to every mortgage company and title insurance agency in the New Jersey area. On the alert it listed our names and stated that we were believed to be involved in fraudulent mortgage lending activities. The alert also stated that anyone who came in contact with any deals that we were involved in should contact agent McCarthy. I received a copy of this alert from a lawyer, David Carmel. He recommended that I retain counsel. I hired Walter Timpone.

In late April, I got a call from my boyfriend at the time, Ronald Dixon, who was a football player for the New York Giants. He sounded disturbed, and he asked that I meet him right away at the Garden State Mall in Paramus, New Jersey. He informed me that the FBI had called the owner of his team and informed him that Dixon's girlfriend (me) was under investigation by the FBI and Dixon should stand clear of me. Directly following, several of my clients and colleagues informed me that they got the same type of calls. Quickly, my reputation and my ability to make money had diminished. At that point, I knew I had to act fast to try and resolve my issues, so I pressed my attorney, Timpone, to schedule a meeting with the U.S. Attorney. Timpone did so.

In early May of 2003, my attorney and I met with U.S. Attorney Michelle Brown, who was assigned to my case. At the meeting with U.S. Attorney Brown, IRS agent Rodriguez and FBI agent Sean McCarthy were present. My attorney, Walter Timpone, proposed a deal requesting that the U.S. Attorney permit me to obtain legitimate financing through my business, Diamond Star Financial, to make the banks whole. The U.S. Attorney agreed, and she gave me a September 1st deadline to obtain financing. As a part of this agreement, I agreed to continue to make the payments on all the loans, to keep them current.

Immediately following, I went to a skilled real estate investor and former banker, Rod Odom, to help secure a lender to finance the properties. Odom had all the properties independently appraised by MIA appraiser Randall Jonason. Jonason appraised the properties to be worth a little over 30 million dollars. After obtaining the appraisals, Odom went to his partner, Donald Roland, who was a banker and CPA, to obtain financing. Odom also arranged a meeting to discuss his financing plan with the U.S. Attorney. At the meeting, U.S. Attorney Michelle Brown, the banks attorneys, Chicago Title's attorneys, Agent McCarthy and Agent Rodriguez were present. Odom detailed his financing strategy and expressed our intention to quickly satisfy all outstanding debts.

During my efforts to obtain financing, The FBI called every contact I had dealt with in the mortgage business, including some of my celebrity clients. Once again, the agent advised these individuals to stand clear of me, because I was under investigation, allegedly for drug dealing, money laundering and other illegal transactions. I was made out to be a figure likened to a member of the drug cartel. Overnight, I was blacklisted by many of my business contacts and clients, who were afraid to deal with me because of the investigation.

I was shocked by the aggressiveness of the investigation in my case, prior to any indictment. While awaiting financing to make the banks whole, my bank account was frozen by the IRS, due to this case. And, my parents' cars, which I had supplied the down payment, were seized that very same day. A swat team of FBI agents surrounded my parents home in Queens, New York at 7:00 am to confiscate their vehicles. My parents, who had worked hard all their lives and never committed any illegal acts, were humiliated. I had supplied the down payment on their cars as a gift. They had no clue that the funds were illegally obtained or they would have never accepted the down payment. My parents were well established, they certainly didn't need my gift. What I thought I was doing as a thoughtful expression of my love turned out to be a curse!

Despite my hardships, I worked hard to get the properties refinanced to make the bank whole. Finally, in late August 2003, I secured a commitment from Roland to close on the properties. Roland met with U.S. Attorney Brown and informed her that he had successfully secured financing and could close the deal within two weeks. I finally thought I would have the opportunity to fix what I had done wrong.

The next afternoon, I received a call from Roland who advised me that he was backing out of the deal. He stated he was called at home by an FBI agent who said he would make Roland's life a "living hell" if he closed this deal. I conferenced my attorney Timpone in on the call with Roland. Timpone immediately reported the agent's adverse conduct to U.S. Attorney Brown and the agent's immediate supervisor.

Unable to convince Roland to close the deal, I was left to go back to the drawing board to seek financing. I was introduced to another mortgage banker, Robert Broit, by my accountant. I met with Broit and provided him with all the documents and information that we used to gain the financing that fell through with Roland. Based on the information Broit received, he felt confident that his private mortgage group would finance the deal. At that point, my attorney arranged for Broit's group to meet with U.S. Attorney Brown.

At the meeting with Broit's representative and the U.S. Attorney, U.S. Attorney Brown stated that I could no longer finance the properties through my business. She said the only way that she would let the transaction close is if the properties were sold to another investor through an arms-length transaction.

Once again, I went back to the drawing table and called every real estate investor that I knew. Out of my calls, I found 4 sets of investors who made offers on the properties. All of the offers went through the U.S. Attorney's office. They were cash offers that ranged up to 26 million dollars. After the buyers were prescreened by the U.S. Attorney's Office, they were turned over to Lehman's attorney, Jeffrey Greenbaum.

To my surprise, Greenbaum's office turned down EVERY offer, including the cash offer presented by Oscar Brown and his group which was for 26 million dollars. Had the bank accepted this offer, ALL the parties involved would have been made WHOLE!

Instead of accepting my investors offers or arranging a public auction of the properties, Greenbaum arranged a private sale of the properties to Lipka Real Estate LLC, owned by one of his colleagues, Chris Lipka, who was a real estate investor that had a vested interest in Lehman. In 2004, Lipka bought all the properties for 14 million dollars. His purchase amount was 3 million dollars LESS than what we originally paid for the properties in 2002, before the biggest real estate boom in recent history, and after over a million dollars of renovations were done on the properties.

After Lehman lawyers sold the properties to their colleague, Lipka, for an upwarded 14 million dollar discount, I was indicted and charged with 7 counts of bank fraud and conspiracy to commit bank fraud. With these charges, I faced up to 30 years in prison.

At that point, my financial situation had drastically changed, so I could no longer afford my high-priced attorney. Therefore, I hired my old attorney, Thomas Nooter, who represented me in my credit fraud case. I explained the details of my case to Nooter and the injustice of the sale of the properties. Nooter advised me that the only way I could expose the bank's wrongdoings and the unjust sale of the properties was to go to trial. He stated, "at this point you have nothing to lose."

CHAPTER FOUR
The Trial

"Shockingly, Infantino testified that 'mistakes' were made on some of the loan files, like submission of two conflicting sets of W2s which would have raised a 'gigantic red flag,' but the deals closed anyway. With these and other problems involved in the underwriting files, the underwriters for Lehman gave Infantino 'ample chances' to fix the problems, which he did."

On September 5, 2007, my trial began in the District Court of New Jersey, before Honorable Jose Linares. From the beginning, we were off to a rocky start. Even though the courthouse was located in the middle of Newark, New Jersey, a predominately African-American area, not one of the jury members on my case was African-American. Furthermore, we only had one African-American to choose from on the entire jury venire, who was ultimately struck by the government during jury selection. My attorney, Thomas Nooter challenged the racial composition of the jury venire. Nooter's argument failed and the trial proceeded.

At my trial, my attorney used a "materiality" defense which he believed to mean: if the bank knew that the documents were fraudulent and did not rely on them to approve the loans, then they were not defrauded. He openly admitted my role in the scheme, but attempted to prove that the bank was involved. This later became a problem.

At the trial, Infantino, testified pursuant to a cooperation agreement reached between he and the government. He admitted that he had been convicted of credit card fraud in 1998 and theft by deception (involving a fraudulent bank loan) in 2005. During cross-examination, Infantino admitted that he had been convicted of possessing cocaine in 2000 and while on probation, he violated the rules of probation by continuing to possess and use drugs. Infantino further admitted that when he applied for his banking license to be a mortgage broker he lied on the application stating he had not been convicted of any crimes whatsoever.

Infantino admitted that I came to him seeking to purchase the house on 497 Piermont Rd, legitimately, in my own name, and he, not I, was the one who devised the scheme with Lehman Brothers Bank. He testified that he personally knew two representatives inside Lehman Brothers Bank named Chris Ridman and Ridman's underwriter, Diane Bauer. He explained how he would submit a fax application to them and that Bauer would fax back a "conditional approval." She would tell him "what he needed to process the loan," including the mortgage application, the bank statements, W2 statements, pay stubs and the contract of sale.

Infantino stated that he did not understand how Goldson, the buyer of 497 Piermont Road, was ultimately approved since a notation in one of the fax communications from Diane Bauer, presented at trial, stated that his credit was not high enough. Infantino admitted that Lehman had provided a set of guidelines as to what was required income and/or asset documentation "needed" for each and every borrower. During cross-examination, Infantino identified several documents from Diane Bauer which instructed him what he needed in order to process the loans. Shockingly, Infantino testified that "mistakes" were made on some of the loan files, like submission of two conflicting sets of W2s which would have raised a "gigantic red flag," but that the deals closed anyway. With these and other problems involved in the underwriting files, the underwriters for Lehman gave Infantino "ample chances" to fix the problems, which he did. Infantino provided mover bills and any documentation required in order to clarify the situation.

Carl Peterson, who was the Senior Vice President for Credit Policy at Aurora Loan Services Inc., testified on behalf of Lehman Brothers Bank FSB. He stated the "mortgage industry" in 2002 was "pretty wild." He added that interest rates were low and that buyers were eager to buy and refinance houses. He further stated that Lehman Brothers issued 22 million dollars in mortgages and recovered, through repossessing and re-selling properties, approximately 10 million dollars. Peterson testified that before entering into contracts with brokers and brokerage companies, Aurora would perform their "due diligence" to determine facts about the mortgage brokers they used. However, in some cases the investigations failed. In the case of Infantino, he admitted that Aurora failed to discover that Infantino, a 25 percent partner in United Mortgage Services, had been convicted of theft by deception and cocaine possession. Both of these facts would have disqualified Infantino from receiving a contract from Aurora Loan Services.

During cross-examination, Peterson was shown an example from the loan portfolio which had been referred for "quality control." Quality control was supposed to be a thorough way of checking the validity and conducting a complete review of the information on the loan application. He noticed that the review included a check of the phone book records to see if the employer of the applicant actually existed. He testified that even though this particular file had been signed off on and had passed quality control inspection, the phone number listed on the file had a different area code then the state of the employer's address. When asked how he thought the file got through quality control with this error, Peterson stated "it must be a typo."

Peterson's testimony ultimately revealed that no "real" checks were performed to verify the information on the loan files. Consequently, the straw buyers were able to close on homes using fictitious job information.

Peterson testified that Aurora was a defendant in civil lawsuits in which they were being sued for failing to accurately evaluate the credit worthiness of mortgages before they issued the loans. He also admitted that Aurora was victimized by 80 bad mortgage loans on high-end properties in Beverly Hills, California. He stated he was also expected to testify in a pending lawsuit about these loans, where a similar scheme was used. He further stated that Aurora had changed its security procedures since the filing of the California lawsuit.

Through trial testimony, it seemed as though my attorney Nooter was able to drive home the point that the bank employees were involved in the scheme. Unfortunately, when the judge rejected Nooter's proposed charge to the jury concerning materiality, we found out that he had misinterpreted the law. The "materiality" defense was measured by a reasonable person standard. Meaning a reasonable person (not a seasoned banker) on plain sight had to view the documents as being illegitimate or phony. Furthermore, according to Third Circuit case law, even if the bank employees were involved in the fraud, their knowledge or involvement is still not a defense to bank fraud. The bank "itself" had to be proven to have been involved in the fraud. At the time of my trial, we only knew that the employees in the bank were involved. We had no idea that the corporate policies of the bank "itself" was predicated on fraudulent lending practices. This information wasn't discovered until after Lehman's collapse on September 15,2008.

Therefore, I went to trial without any real defense, so I was doomed! Consequently, on September 20,2007, just hours after jury deliberation began, I was convicted on all charged counts.

Prior to my sentencing, I was advised by another attorney that I should get appraisals on all the properties and a detailed title report tracking ownership, along with an evaluation of the bank's appraisals and their sale to Lipka. As suggested, I obtained these reports. I hired two separate MIA appraisers. One of them was Randall Jonason who originally appraised the properties for Odom in 2003. Jonason's evaluation concluded that at the time of Lehman's sale to Lipka the properties were worth more than 7 million dollars more than what was owed to the bank. He stated in his report that the sale to Lipka, a Lehman insider, "defied logic." Additionally, the title report revealed that the properties were resold for millions of dollars in profit! These documents were included in my sentencing memorandum, but my attorney did not formally object to the loss amount on record, as required by law. Mistakenly, he only used the documents as an argument for a downward departure. He later admitted his mistake to the Third Circuit Court of Appeals in my direct appeal.

The end result, on July 16, 2008 I was sentenced to 12 1/2 years in prison, largely based on the large loss amount that the bank "itself" derived. My sentence was calculated according to the U.S. Federal Sentencing Guidelines, which increases the time a person serves based on the loss amount derived in the case. Had the bank accepted the legitimate offers made on the properties, my sentence would have been approximately 24 months.

Infantino, the mortgage banker who admitted that he orchestrated the scheme and got each deal approved through his inside contact in the bank, was sentenced to 24 months in prison. His sentence ran concurrent with an additional sentence that was imposed on him by the State of New Jersey, stemming from his participation in another large mortgage fraud case that involved the identity theft of disabled people. The lawyer, Daniel Ellis who prepared the fraudulent mortgage documents, and who secured the money from Lehman, also got a 24 month sentence. Both Infantino and Ellis were middle aged white men, who were seasoned veterans in the mortgage industry and both had a history of prior fraudulent dealings. Without these key figures the loans in my case would have never been able to close.

To date, I have served 5 years in prison, and I still have 7 1/2 years left to serve on my sentence. I am the first one to admit that my actions were wrong, and I should have been punished for what I did. I deserved to go to prison, but I believe the sentence I received was extremely harsh, especially considering the circumstance. I have been severely punished for my role in this scheme, yet not one Lehman director or employee has served a day of prison time. Is that fair?

CHAPTER FIVE
Life In Prison

"I've learned the hard way that all crime results in negative consequences, so I've vowed to deter from crime at all cost!"

Despite the hand that I was dealt, I have worked vigorously to make the best out of my current situation. During my imprisonment I have proactively worked on making wiser decisions and becoming a better person. Stripped of my finances and my prestige, I was forced to deal with the root of my dilemma- myself. No longer able to hide behind people, places and things, I had to go within to find my own inner strengths and weaknesses. On my path to self-discovery, I had to learn how to love myself and forgive myself for my past actions. It took years to rid myself of shame and guilt and to admit my own faults. But when I did, I finally felt empowered! I was excited to share the road map I used with the many downtrodden women who I was surrounded by. Just like myself, these women suffered from low self-esteem and used external props to determine their self-worth. With the help of family and friends, I was able to publish a three book series, entitled the "Voices of Consequences Enrichment Series." My books are geared to empower incarcerated women to heal, recognize their potential and recapture their dreams.

Women all across the country have said that my books have been essential in helping them overcome their dilemmas. I have had no greater professional achievement then to see the fruit of my labor through these women's testimonies. I have learned from this experience that despite being in a dark place in my own life, I can still make a difference.

While incarcerated, I joined a public speaking group called C.H.O.I.C.E.S. administered by our prison camp administrator. Through this group, I have frequently gone out into the community to speak to youth about the bad choices I made that led to my imprisonment. This past November, our group was given an award by the U.S. Attorney's Office in the District of Connecticut for our outstanding work in the community. In front of a packed audience at Yale University's Sprague Hall, I stood and gave an acceptance speech on behalf of our group. We received a standing ovation. At that moment, it registered in my mind the extent of the impact that lessons from real life stories can have on our youth. Hearing my story and others similar to mine, many youth have vowed not to take the route that we once took. This experience inspired me to create a cautionary tale about my early life entitled, "She's All Caught Up." My memoir details the influences and poor choices I made as a youth, which formed my negative thinking patterns, and the high price I had to pay for my bad choices. Not only do I think my books will help incarcerated women, from the response I received from my public speaking in the community, I believe they will have an even bigger impact on teens and "at-risk" youth.

I've learned the hard way that all crime results in negative consequences, so I've vowed to deter from crime at all cost! One of my biggest regrets in life was quitting school to pursue business opportunities. I no longer wanted to live with regrets, so I've decided not to take any more short-cuts and to utilize my time of imprisonment to pursue my education. I am currently working hard to earn my Bachelor's degree, behind bars.

My successful reformation in prison would not be possible without the support of my family. Prior to my imprisonment, I failed to see the strength of their love and loyalty to me. Sad to say, in many ways when things were going well in my life I neglected them and took them for granted. When the prison bars shut behind me, many of the people for whom I had done the most and tried so hard to please turned their backs on me. Like the old saying: Out of sight, out of mind. The opposite occurred with my parents: My imprisonment has made our relationship grow stronger. They have truly weathered the storm!

My parents have successfully tackled the job of helping to raise my two teenage children. Life for my children hasn't been easy without the presence of their mom. My parents have done the best they could to keep my kids upbeat and have helped them to heal from the traumatic experiences they have gone through, due to my absence. Not only have my parents picked up my responsibility of raising my children, they were also left to pay my debts.

While imprisoned my parents lost a civil lawsuit against them initiated by Lehman. They were accused of conversion under New Jersey state law. Under this law, even if a person did not know that he or she received money gained from illegal proceeds the fact that the money passed through their accounts is enough to hold them liable in a civil suit. Back in 2002, I asked my parents to hold money for me in their savings account that I didn't want to spend frivolously. I wrote them a check, never thinking any harm would result from my actions. In spring of 2002, when I agreed at the U.S. Attorney's office to pay the monthly mortgage payments to Lehman, my parents returned the money to me, which was all documented through checks and wires. And I used the money to pay the mortgages, so it ultimately went back to Lehman. Nonetheless, my parents were sued and a $400,000 judgment was placed against them. My parents, who are now retired, had to mortgage their home, which they had just paid off, to settle this debt that I ultimately caused.

Instead of being angry with me, as I thought they would be, my parents have supported me wholeheartedly. The week after the judgment was finalized against them, they came to visit me in prison. I knew for sure they would yell at me for my poor judgments, but they didn't. I'll never forget my mother's heartfelt words. "As long as we have each other, we have everything we need. We don't care about no money. We care about you," she said passionately as I broke down in tears. Her words made me reflect. In the past I was driven by money and prestige, and in the end none of those things mattered. Today I know I have what's important. I have real love.

To help support my mission, my parents created Voices International Publications Inc. as a vehicle to publish my books and help other incarcerated women. Out of their retirement fund and with the help of a few family friends, they have donated my books to imprisoned women across the country. My mother also started an email service that sends daily inspirations and a weekly resource list to these women. My parents kindness and unconditional love has inspired me to do everything possible to turn my life around and make them proud of me. They have led by example and taught me not to just "talk the talk, but to walk the walk." Today they aren't just my parents, they are my best friends.

With the hopes of gaining my freedom and returning home to my family, I have persistently studied the law. While imprisoned at the Danbury FCI, I learned about the Federal Sentencing Guidelines and how the loss amount in white collar cases is calculated. Through my research, I discovered that my attorney, Nooter, failed to challenge properly the loss amount in my case and to contest that the full loss was not caused by my conduct, as required for enhancement according to the guidelines. I provided this information to Nooter during the time he was preparing my direct appeal. He admitted his error in my direct appeal and challenged the loss amount calculation for the first time in my reply brief. Unfortunately his efforts were "too late." The Third Circuit Court of Appeals ruled that he could not address this issue for the first time in a reply brief, so the argument was never ruled on.

As a pro se litigant, I have continued to fight my case. To date, I have not been successful, but I do believe one day justice will be rendered. Therefore, I refuse to let go of my faith.

I have now shared with you my story, my faults and my vulnerabilities. This wasn't an easy process. No one wants to share their wrongdoings and their character flaws. I am no different. I have stepped out of the closet of shame with hope that someone who reads my story will help me in my plight to freedom. Even if it is just a kind word that will help to champion me on my journey, your words will be greatly appreciated.

The question that still remains unanswered is: Should savvy Wall Street bankers be allowed to retain the large dividends they made that resulted in the 2008 Financial Crisis and escape punishment? And should "small fries" like myself be left to do big time? You be the judge!

THE HIGH PRICE I HAD TO PAY

AFTERWORD

To date, I have been incarcerated for close to seven years; I never believed in a million years I'd have the strength to endure this journey, but by God's grace, He has kept me. After writing "The High Price I Had To Pay" back in 2013, I mustered the courage to send a copy of my book to every judge on the Third Circuit Court of Appeals. I believed if the Court could see I had the ability to effectively express what happened to me in writing, justice would finally be rendered on my behalf. After utilizing my father's pension funds to retain a high-powered attorney who I believed would help me and then being abandoned by this attorney, despite the fact he was paid a hefty retainer, I had no choice but to fight my legal battle pro se. With the help of an ex-federal attorney and an ex-state senator, I sent a passionate letter to the Chief Judge and all the panel judges. I expressed I was not representing myself pro se by choice, but because it was my only means of obtaining relief after my attorney ran off with my retainer. In the correspondence I included a copy of my book and a copy of my recent judgment I won against John Jay Fahy, my former attorney, which was issued by the N.J. Ethics Fee Arbitration Committee. I pleaded for the Court's mercy and asked for their help. I believed if the judges saw the full picture they would help me. I was wrong! My motion was denied by both the Court of Appeals and the Supreme Court. With that last denial, I was left with no further legal recourse.

The events that took place shortly after blew my mind! I felt like I was an involuntary cast member in a thrilling horror movie. On July 17, 2013, just 3 days prior to his scheduled license suspension date for nonpayment of the judgment I won against him, my former attorney John Jay Fahy killed himself on one of the busiest highways in New Jersey. It was hard to comprehend why a prominent attorney who was a former Assistant United Sates Attorney, the former chief prosecutor of Bergen County and a MSNBC news analyst would kill himself. I refused to believe my $44,000 judgment was the cause of his death. This event raised my suspicions about what was really going on in my case, and who the real players were.

For months I remained flooded with inner turmoil. I felt helpless, yet something inside of me refused to give up. Previously it was my belief that Lehman Brothers Bank was the main culprit in my case. I believed the bankers used their power to influence the Government, resulting in my lengthy sentence. It was after the infamous Bridgegate scandal that my point of view was significantly altered. It came to light that the key players who were involved in my prosecution were all woven together through their professional careers and personal relationships. Although this may be common in law and politics, the many conflicts of interest clearly posed problems in my case.

Christopher J. Christie, the current Governor of New Jersey, was the U.S. Attorney who presided over my case. On my sentencing date he released a statement, "This is a long prison sentence that appropriately matched the breadth and complexity of the fraud committed by Davis." I never understood why the Government was going so hard and making me out as a mastermind of a crime that clearly took the help of insiders. Although I knew I was a target of an over-zealous FBI agent, who had me arrested several times on fictitious charges which were later dropped, I had no clue the corrupt government officials may have also played a role in my demise. It was never clear why the Government would allow Lehman attorneys to accept an offer from an inside investor for at least a $12 million discount, especially when offers were prescreened by the U.S. Attorney's office that would have made the bank whole. After reading a stack of articles about the Bridgegate scandal, the incident that alleged Christie's administration ordered the shut down of three lanes on the Fort Lee entrance of the George Washington Bridge in retribution to the Fort Lee Mayor for not endorsing Christie's re-election campaign, I quickly recognized the name of key players from my case, including my former attorney. Article after article detailed corruption, bullying and underhanded deals that Christie and his camp were a part of, which resembled the same behavior that took place in my case. I felt it was important to share some of the details of what I discovered in this revised edition to shed light on the character of those involved in the prosecution against me and their relationship to one another. I believe these key factors may have attributed to the injustices I encountered.

* * *

The first of my research led me to learn about the many allegations of misconduct by my former U.S. Attorney, now N.J. Governor Christie. I found it hard to stomach the many scandals he was alleged to be a part of in the media as I related each of them to similar events that took place in my case. Christie, a political tycoon, clearly had a focus. It was his dream to reign in politics, even as a young child. The many articles I read presented him as a relentless bully, willing to do whatever it took to climb the ladder of politics. It was shocking to learn Christie won his first election back in 1994, which was for a seat on the Board of Chosen Freeholders in Morris County, using unscrupulous tactics. According to legal documents, in the final weekend before the Republican primary, Christie released an ad charging that three of his opponents in the nine-person Republican primary were being "investigated by the Morris County prosecutor." This was a serious allegation that happened to also be false. Christie ultimately won the primary and the general election, but his win came at a large price. He was successfully sued for defamation of character by the three victims of his false ad. As a part of the settlement Christie was forced to apologize to all three victims in local newspapers. Two years later he lost his seat.

To understand the web of politics I had unknowingly been intertwined in, I had to study the players and their rise to power. I learned that Christie's career in politics took off in 1992, after he volunteered for George W. Bush's campaign. He met Bill Palatucci, who was the executive director of both Bush's Presidential campaigns in New Jersey. After Bush lost the election, Christie convinced Palatucci to become partners with him in his firm. It was said to be a trade off. Christie agreed to teach Palatucci everything he knew about practicing law, and Palatucci taught Christie all about politics.

In mid-2000 when Bush's victory seemed plausible, Christie became interested in the job as U.S. Attorney for New Jersey. Although Christie had no prior criminal or prosecutorial experience, with Palatucci's backing and a letter of support from former Governor Thomas Kean, Christie made the cut. The politics of 9/11 helped secure the deal. Bush had an approved rate of ninety per cent, so Democrats had no interest in fighting Bush's choice for the position.

The articles I read detail that during his reign as New Jersey U.S. Attorney, Christie prosecuted dozens of "corrupt" political figures. He used his power to make strategic alliances, awarding those who helped him in the past and punishing those who stood against him. For instance, in 2005 George Norcross III, who is said to be New Jersey's most influential Democratic politicians, was under investigation after a South Jersey town councilman wore a wire and recorded hours of conversations with Norcross. Allegedly, although the tapes contained damaging information that inferred extortion, Christie opted not to pursue Norcross. Instead, in January of 2009, he wrote a six-page letter to the state attorney general stating he opted not to indict Norcross because the investigation had been mishandled. In turn, he aligned himself with one of the most influential Democrats in the state. Ultimately, this relationship, and similar alliances, are said to have helped Christie win office as Governor of New Jersey, a state that traditionally consisted primarily of Democrats.

From reading the articles about Christie and his tenure at the U.S. Attorney's office, I learned prosecution is not about the crime you commit or justice. In Christie's case, it seemed to be all about politics. If you're connected and can be beneficial later on, you got a pass. If not, you're toast! This even proved to be true in the case of his brother, Todd Christie. Remember I mentioned on my sentencing date Christie stated, that my 12 1/2 year sentence for bank fraud "appropriately matches the breadth and complexity of the fraud." It was a different story when it came to his brother's documented wrong doings that far exceeded the complexity of my case. Despite being found by the SEC to have made 1,600 illegal trades between 1999-2003, bilking investors in excess of $1.6 million, which he personally netted, Todd Christie avoided indictment. SEC civil case filings revealed that Todd Christie and 14 other specialists defrauded investors of approximately $19 million, which greatly exceeds the loss created in my case, yet Todd Christie was never prosecuted for his role in the scheme. Even more interesting, criminal charges were brought against a selection of those involved. Three of the individuals charged had greater culpability than Todd, and 11 had less. One of the individuals was alleged to have only profited $14,000 from the scheme. They were all indicted in the Southern District of New York, under the supervision of then U.S. Attorney David Kelly. Kelly was reportedly behind the decision that allowed Todd to escape criminal liability. Not long after Todd Christie's potential criminal liability was laid to rest, David Kelly received a multimillion dollar, no bid, monitoring contract from Christie himself, which again raised concerns in the media with no repercussions for Christie.

Reading this information only reassured me there are severe double standards when it comes to prosecution in the United States judicial system. U.S. Attorneys are given a tremendous amount of power, even more than federal judges. They have the ability to decide who gets prosecuted and who does not. In addition, they decide what charges will be brought up against the accused, which ultimately determines how much time the individual will serve if convicted. In essence, they play a role comparable to God when it concerns someone's fate in the judicial process.

It was disheartening to learn about the character of the god-like figures connected to my case, including Christie. Not only did the articles reveal Christie was strategic and calculated against those whom he choose to, or not to, prosecute, but he also has been heavily criticized for rewarding his friends and those who do his dirty work for him, often at the expense of those he prosecuted. For instance, while Christie was the U.S. Attorney he conducted a criminal investigation against Zimmer Holdings concerning kickbacks by knee and hip replacement manufacturers. This probe was settled for $311 million, of which $52 million of the settlement went to Christie's old boss, former Attorney General John Ashcroft. Although it was cited that Ashcroft had no prior experience in this field, at the direction of Christie, Zimmer Holdings hired Ashcroft's consulting firm to monitor its compliance with the settlement. This arrangement caught the attention of Congress, causing Christie to be hauled before a House subcommittee during his gubernatorial campaign to testify about the deal.

Page after page, I learned about the underhanded deals that took place as common practice in N.J. politics. Even Christie's wife, Mary Pat seemed to benefit from his seat in office. After a deal was brokered with Angelo Gordon Investment firm to manage the state's pension funds, Mary Pat was hired in 2012 by the firm, which paid her $475,000 a year. The media criticized the relationship with the Governor's wife and this firm, which to

42

date has been paid more that $11.8 million in fees. Even though Mary Pat was hired a year after New Jersey stopped investing with Angelo Gordon, according to a spokesperson from the N.J. Treasury Department, the state is still paying the firm hundreds of thousands of dollars because the state continues to hold an "illiquid" investment in the firm, valued at $6.6 million.

Clearly understanding the political culture and the fact Christie seems to be all about money, my mind began to wonder about the properties in question in my case. I couldn't help but wonder who really benefitted from the equity in the properties taken that was upward $12 million according to two MIA appraisals? And, what deal was cut to block my legal efforts to ensure my case never resurfaced?

* * *

The next part of my research led me to discover my original attorney, Walter Timpone, who helped arrange meetings with the proposed buyers of the properties and the U.S. Attorney's office, and who conveniently loss all the files that contained the details of those meetings, is also a close ally of Christie. According to the New York Times, Timpone, who served at the U.S. Attorney's office for 11 years, was slated to be the first assistant to New Jersey's United States Attorney. His appointment was a recommendation of then state Senators, Robert G. Torricelli and Jon S. Corzine. Both senators agreed not to challenge President Bush's appointment of Christopher Christie, who at the time had no prior experience conducting criminal investigations, if Timpone would be appointed second in command. To their dismay, Timpone's appointment did not clear the Justice Department because of an F.B.I. background check. In 2001, Timpone was accused of meddling in a F.B.I sting aimed at then state Senator Torricelli, the same senator who endorsed him for the position of second in command at the U.S. Attorney's office.

According to F.B.I records, at the time Timpone was representing Robert Janiszewski, a Hudson County executive who was a friend and political supporter of Torricelli. Agents attempted to get Janiszewski to wear a wire and help gather evidence against the senator. Although Timpone assured prosecutors he had no conflict of interest and did not share a close relationship with the senator, the F.B.I. agents conducting surveillance on Torricelli's home later saw Timpone visit the senator. Prosecutors on the case were so incensed they considered filing criminal and ethical charges against Timpone for impeding a federal investigation. This incident appeared in Timpone's F.B.I. background check, delaying his appointment. In attempt to revive the candidacy, Christie flew to Washington D.C. to met with Justice Department officials on Timpone's behalf. In addition, Christie made a public statement in support of Timpone, stating, "Wally Timpone is of great integrity who once served this office well."

Reading this information, I felt like such a fool! I certainly had not done my homework before hiring Timpone. How could I expect him to fairly represent me when he had such allegiance to the government players who seemed to turn a "blind eye" to Lehman's inside fraud? Ultimately Timpone's loyalty to his peers did not pay off for me, but it certainly helped him!

In 2010, Timpone was handpicked by Christie to be the Vice Chairman of the N.J. Election Law Enforcement Commission (ELEC). His name later resurfaced during the Bridgegate scandal. Timpone initially represented Bridget Kelly, who was the former deputy chief of staff for legislative and intergovernmental affairs in Christie's office. It was Kelley's emails that were intercepted, indicating she instructed David Wildstein, who was the Governor's second-highest appointee at the Port Authority, to engineer the traffic jam, allegedly as reattribution to the Fort Lee mayor who refused to endorse Christie.

* * *

As I sifted further through the articles, I recognized another name in Christie's entourage that continuously appeared, Michele Brown. She was the original Assistant U.S. Attorney assigned to my case. Under her watch, she helped Lehman attorney's acquire the properties back in my case, without proper foreclosure, through strong arm tactics. Additionally, she personally prescreened all the buyers I brought to the table. Ultimately, she was the government referee who allowed Lehman attorneys to sell the properties to a vested investor for a $14 million discount, even though she personally interviewed cash buyers who made offers that were up to $12 million greater than the accepted offer. The offers presented would have in fact made the bank whole.

Through the articles, I learned on August 18, 2009, Chris Christie acknowledged he loaned $46,000 to Brown in 2007, while serving as her superior at the U.S. Attorney's office. According to the New York Times, Christie failed to report either the loan or its monthly $500 interest payments on both his income tax returns and his mandatory financial disclosure report to the New Jersey Election Law Enforcement Commission. When the news broke about the loan, Christie stated he was merely helping a friend in need, and Brown had done nothing to help his gubernatorial campaign. Yet, the evidence showed differently.

Under Christie's watch, Brown was promoted to become Acting First Assistant U.S. Attorney. In March 2009, after Christie's departure to run for Governor, Brown interceded in a Freedom of Information Act (FOIA) request which was initiated by the then N.J. Governor Jon S. Corzine. Utilizing her position of power, according to federal law enforcement officials in Newark and Washington, Brown took over for the staff member who normally oversaw FOIA requests. It was assumed this was an attempt to intercept the requests which included records about Christie's travel and expenses, along with Brown's travel records.

In October 2009, the Associated Press obtained travel records revealing Christie "regularly spent beyond federal guidelines on business travel while he was U.S. Attorney, including $400 per night stays at luxury hotels. During trips he took in 2007 and 2008, the AP reported that Brown "also exceeded the guidelines after Christie approved her requests for rooms in the same five-star hotels where he was booked."

Additionally, it was discovered in mid-June 2009, according to a New York Times article, when F.B.I. agents and prosecutors gathered to set a date for the arrests of more than 40 targets of a corruption and money laundering probe, Brown argued for the arrests to be made before July. According to three federal law enforcement officials briefed on the conversation, she later told colleagues she wanted to ensure the arrests occurred before Christie's permanent successor took office, presumably so that Christie would be given credit for the round up.

When the news about the loan scandal and the arrests to help his gubernatorial campaign came to light in the media, Brown resigned from the U.S. Attorney's office, stating she did not want to "become a distraction." In September 2009, Brown started working at the law firm of McElroy, Deutsch, Mulvaney & Carpenter, which is the same law firm my first attorney Walter Timpone worked for.

Christie did not forget Brown's loyalty. When the press died down, in January 2010, Governor-elect Christie named Brown as his appointments counsel to join his senior staff. Through the position she was in charge of job placements as well as recruiting and guiding nominees for cabinet-level and judicial posts.

Once her loyalty was further proven, in October 2012, Christie appointed Brown to become the chief executive officer of the N.J. Economic Development Authority (EDA). During that time, the EDA administered $460 million of federal funds for Hurricane Sandy relief, including the controversial ad campaign "Stronger Than The Storm." Christie's endorsement of Brown as CEO of the EDA was highly criticized in the media. Critics contended she lacked experience in business development, marketing or tourism, which encompassed a major component of her job duties that included overseeing the state's multimillion dollar economic development programs. Furthermore, the former CEO of EDA made $186,600 a year. Yet, Brown's salary was $225,000 a year and required a co-president and chief operating officer, whose salary was an additional $201,000 yearly, to assist her, due to her lack of experience. Nonetheless, her appointment was finalized and she continued to show her alliance to Christie.

In March 2013, as a part of her job as the CEO of the EDA, Brown became a ranking administration official on the state contract selection committee. Her vote on a five panel member committee to approve the controversial "Stronger Than The Storm" ad campaign, which featured Christie and his immediate family swimming at the Jersey shore became a hot topic in the media. It was said the ad, which was paid for with federal funds from the Sandy Relief Fund, was used to help promote Christie's reelection campaign. Even more shocking, the bid was won by an advertising group, MWW group, that submitted a bid for $2.2 million above what was sought by the other finalist. According to the evaluation sheets of the advertisement bid, Brown gave MWW a score that was above even the high average score the company received overall. An investigation was launched about the misuse of Sandy Relief Funds, and Christie's executive ties to the MWW group and influence on the bid, putting Brown back in the highlight of the media.

Most recently in February 2015, it was reported Christie was at the center of a new federal investigation also involving Brown. Back in 2010, Christie's administration allegedly quashed 43 indictments of Hunterdon County law enforcement agents, including the then Sheriff and Undersheriff of the town. They were accused of attempting to hire under-qualified officers, demanding loyalty oaths from employees and permitting the distribution of unauthorized sheriff's IDs for politically connected friends of the department. The Christie administration allegedly stepped in, had the indictments overturned, and ousted the two prosecutors who brought the charges. At first, the Governor's office stated in October 2013 that the Governor "had no knowledge whatsoever of the case in question, its prosecution or ultimate dismissal by the judge." Yet, just last week, one of the prosecutors whom they ousted, Barlyn, filed a civil suit that revealed Christie's immediate entourage, including Brown, in fact had knowledge of the events. His filing included a series of emails that showed Dermot O'Grady, a Christie administration deputy attorney general who was tasked with taking over the Hunterdon prosecutor's office, received an email from Michele Brown, who had some questions concerning Barlyn and the indictments. That email dated September 17, 2010 was also sent to O'Grady's direct supervisor, Stephen Taylor of the N.J. Attorney General's Division of Criminal Justice in Trenton, prior to the quashed indictment. Brown's email is now the link that connects Christie to this scandal, which is a part of a new federal investigation.

* * *

As I continued to dive into the large stack of articles that read like an episode of CSI, my heart began to race. How could I ever expect to receive justice in a system run by people who had more power, skills and courage than veteran mobsters?

The next set of articles I read left me lost for words. My final shot at justice was my Motion 2255 to Vacate, Set Aside, or Correct my sentence, which was filed in late 2010. I had gathered all the evidence I needed to show that my attorney was ineffective. I believed, at least, I would be granted an evidentiary hearing. Backed by the ruling of the Third Circuit Court Of Appeals, in the denial of my direct appeal, that blatantly said my attorney did not comply with the rules of the Court to address my most important issue on loss amount, and with the bank's collapse and exposure of massive fraudulent conduct, I didn't think the Government would challenge my motion. I was wrong! Donna Gallucio, who was my Assistant United States Attorney, went hard to block my efforts to obtain relief, with disregard for the law.

Reading the articles, I also found out Gallucio was rewarded for her loyalty to Christie. In September 2010, she was nominated by Governor Christie to be a Superior Court Judge. On October 3, 2011, she was sworn in at a ceremony that Christie attended. Today she is a Superior Court Judge in the Criminal Division of Superior Court in Passaic County, primarily due to the support of Christie.

* * *

The last of my research led me back to my Judge, Honorable Jose Linares. He is a Cuban American whose family escaped Cuba in 1965 when he was 12. Linares was a star player on his high school football team, and recruited to play for Jersey City State, now New Jersey City University, as a linemen. The quarterback for his college team was Joe DiVincenzo, the Essex County executive, who some consider the most powerful Democrat in North Jersey. Although DiVincenzo is a Democrat he has maintained a close friendship with Linares. Even more interesting, several of the articles I read tied DiVincenzo as a mutual friend of Christie. DiVincenzo's relationship with Christie began after the F.B.I. raided the office where he worked and Christie cleared his name. A letter was written to DiVincenzo's lawyer, which stated he was "not a subject or target of the grand jury investigation." Later, DiVincenzo became a de facto lobbyist to help Christie push for stricter rules on arbitration awards for police and fire union contracts. According to reports, Christie rewarded DiVincenzo with influence and funds for a new senior center in Belleville,

$4 million to finance a new technology wing at the Essex County Vocational Center and $7 million in Port Authority funds for a new waterfront park in Newark. DiVincenzo returned the favor by publicly endorsing Christie's reelection.

Even after the state's Election Law Enforcement Commission charged DiVincenzo with using his campaign account for personal items, such as trips to Puerto Rico and gym memberships, Christie still praised DiVincenzo and refused to distance himself. This showed me they all had an inseparable bond of allegiance to one another, which I certainly could not pierce even with the law on my side.

Not only did I find out my Judge's long term friend and college pal, DiVincenzo, had ties to Christie, so does his good friend Bill Palatucci who helped him gain his spot on the bench. It was Linares's ties to both the Hispanic legal community and the state's Republicans that boosted his career. Linares was appointed as a judge back in 2002, by George W. Bush. This was the same year that Bush appointed Christopher Christie as U.S. Attorney. Palatucci was the executive director of both Bush's Presidential campaigns and Christie's law partner, who also assisted Christie with gaining his position in office. He is also the same political figure that helped my Judge, Honorable Jose Linares in receiving his judgeship that same year.

Most recently, Palatucci and Christie were the center of a scandal regarding the shoddy oversight of New Jersey halfway houses, which were allegedly packed to increase revenue for a private prison organization Palatucci headed. According to a series of articles in the New York Times, during Christie's first 39 months in office, more than 1,000 prisoners escaped these facilities that are supposed to serve as low security rehabilitation centers for minor offenders. One of the escapees murdered a young woman which brought the halfway houses, referred to as "dumping grounds" for all kinds of prisoners, under scrutiny. During the investigation it was discovered Palatucci is the Vice

President of Community Education Centers, the company that received the bulk of the state's budget for halfway houses. It was also noted that back in the 90's both Christie and Palatucci worked as lobbyists for this same company. Christie's praise of the facilities, despite their known recent issues, has prompted state senate hearings.

* * *

Putting together the pieces of the puzzle made me understand why despite my numerous valid legal arguments presented to the courts, I never stood a chance to win. All the players in my case were deeply connected, and none of them were willing to sink the other on behalf of justice.

While sitting on the top of my bunk bed in federal prison, where I am serving a decade plus sentence, I realized my sentence is longer than any convicted top ranking banker including Charles Keating, who was the star of the Savings & Loan scandal back in the 80's that bilked thousands of investors out of billions of dollars. The true culprits are living "high on the hog," and they are being rewarded for their relentless misdeeds.

It was important for me to tell this new part of my story and shed light on the power of the U.S. justice system and those who run it. When power is given to individuals who lack character and integrity they often misuse it to benefit themselves, which may cause significant harm to others. For close to seven years, I've been blocked on every side from having my case heard by an unbiased party that is not a part of the Christie camp. It's not until recently that I recognized the real Goliath that I may have been fighting against, due to the many smoke screens my powerful opponent used as distractions. What I do know for sure, I am not being punished for my crime. I am a true political prisoner; an enemy of the Christie camp!

I don't have a bunch of money, nor do I have the power or prestige to fight the Taliban that has joined forces against me. Yet, like David, I do have a ton of faith in God and I have my writing pen. I will use these weapons to fight against injustice and shed light on the abuse of power that has become common in our Justice system, which lacks a reliable watch dog system to oversea those who have been granted a tremendous amount of power and influence.

It is my hope with this updated edition of my book, I will finally get my case in front of an entity that will help. It's certainly been a long time coming, but I do believe in my heart my change will come!

Articles Written In Her Fight Against Injustice

Written by: Jamila T. Davis

"Behind bars I've used my ability to write to expose injustices within the U.S. judicial system and to rally for reform. I believe a fool simply complains but does not act to create change. I realized without the voices of those who have been done wrong, people will not know about the pain that we have endured. Therefore, I made it a point to use one of the only weapons I have as an incarcerated woman in my effort to make a difference; I use my pen!"

JUSTICE IN DENIAL: A PRISONER'S WORST NIGHTMARE

Written by: Jamila T. Davis

I stood frozen in disbelief as I read the email my mother had sent, over and over. Goosebumps flooded over my arms and chills went up my spine, once reality settled in. I couldn't believe my former attorney, John Jay Fahy, was dead. At first, I felt a sense of guilt. I was torn between anger and remorse, struggling with the thought that my fight for freedom may somehow have been related. As a federal prisoner sentenced to 12 1/2 years for bank fraud, with 7 1/2 years left to serve on my sentence, this tragic news was yet another curve ball in my case.

Just 3 days before the New Jersey Supreme Court was scheduled to suspend Fahy's license for his failure to return $44,000 of the $50,000 retainer that his firm received to represent me, Fahy shot and killed himself. On a sidewalk along Route 17, one of the busiest and most visible highways in New Jersey, his body laid lifeless, backing up traffic for hours. Clearly he had the need to send a message...But what was it?

In 2007, after I was convicted by jury for bank fraud, I was introduced to John Jay Fahy by Alfred Decotiis- a prominent attorney heavily involved in New Jersey politics. Witnessing Judge Jose Linares' almost star struck reaction to Alfred Decotiis who made a brief appearance at my trial in the Newark, New Jersey District Courthouse, I figured reaching back out to Decotiis would be a good idea. After explaining to him my legal dilemmas and my need for effective legal representation, he referred me to Fahy.

Taking Decotiis' advice, I eagerly reached out to Fahy, a former U.S. attorney and white collar crime specialist who made frequent television appearances as a legal analyst. I explained my complex case to Fahy, which involved 7 high-end properties in Alpine and Saddle River, New Jersey, financed by Lehman Brothers Bank. During the meeting with Fahy I detailed the numerous attempts I made to pay off the loans in question which would have made the banks whole. However, instead of accepting full price offers on the properties, all of which were prescreened and approved through the U.S. Attorney's office by former AUSA Michelle Brown, Lehman Brothers' attorney, Jeffrey Greenbaum, made the decision to sell the properties to an inside investor, Chris Lipka, for a substantial discount. As a part of a "sweet-heart" deal, Lipka received 9 properties which were skillfully negotiated and purchased in 2002 for 17 million dollars, through distressed property sales. During the largest real estate boom in recent history and after several million dollars in renovations on these prime estates, Lipka purchased the properties in 2004 for 14 million dollars. This purchase price was nearly half of the properties appraised value! I explained to Fahy that my argument was not whether or not I was guilty. I knew my involvement in the Lehman financing scheme was wrong, and I admitted my misconduct from the very beginning. My main issue concerned the loss that was created in my case, which was not attributed to my conduct or the conduct of my codefendants. I argued that the bank itself caused the loss by selling the properties for a huge discount to an investor who was vested in Lehman. This was all revealed through civil proceedings in my case. (See Lehman Brothers Bank FSB v. Ellis et al., Docket No. ESX-C-103-03 (NJ Superior Court, Essex County)). At the time, I knew federal white collar sentences were based largely on loss amount. The larger the loss, the larger the sentence. Therefore, I sought Fahy's assistance in reducing the loss amount.

I also detailed to Fahy my several prior arrests based on fictitious charges, which were orchestrated by agent Sean McCarthy- the lead agent on my case. I explained how I spent many years and my last dollars fighting baseless legal battles, most of which were eventually dismissed, all incited by Agent McCarthy. (See Davis v. McCarthy, et al. Civil Action No. 12-429 (JLL) N.J.D.C). I asked for Fahy's help with getting one of these frivolous cases dismissed. In this case, I was accused of false impersonation and stealing the identity of Sebastian Volterelli, a white Italian male. Agent Sean McCarthy and former Bergen County Detective Nieciecki used false information to obtain an arrest warrant and a search warrant to enter my house. As a result, I was arrested and held on a 1 million dollar cash bond, for something I didn't do. Although agent McCarthy and Nieciecki received a confession from Volterelli that his identity was never stolen, during my incarceration, both officers acted in concert and hid this information from the prosecutor. Consequently, I sat in jail on frivolous charges for 3 months. When I was finally released after posting a substantial bail, I was also placed on 24 hour house arrest for 18 months, until my sentencing in federal court. (See NJ Crim. Complaint No. W2006-337-290 Bergen County, NJ.).

Once Fahy heard my story, he felt confident that he could help me. His firm received a $50,000 retainer, which was paid out of my father's retirement account, to assist with the preparation of my presentence report and to prepare an appeal on my behalf for the New Jersey District Court case. He also agreed to assist in getting the charges on the bogus Bergen County case dismissed. In anticipation of effective results, I agreed to his terms of assistance.

At first Fahy seemed enthusiastic about helping me. He appeared friendly, warm and smart. From the onset, he came up with some good strategies for sentencing. He stated that we needed to order two separate independent appraisals on the houses along with title reports to show that the sale of the properties was not an "arms-length" transaction. He also stated that with the several dismissed charges and documented harassment by the agent, we would be able to support our claim of government misconduct, and substantially bolster my case. He advised with this evidence I would be looking at a maximum of three years in prison. I quickly followed Fahy's lead and got the documentation that he requested. Fahy worked along with my former attorney, Thomas Nooter, who did all of the written work. Fahy became the coach that directed Nooter on what to do. I felt secure knowing that regardless of the outcome at sentencing, Fahy would prepare an appeal on my behalf.

My sentencing was scheduled for July 16, 2008. To my surprise, I was sentenced to 12 1/2 years in prison. I immediately thought something had gone drastically wrong! In Essex County jail I phoned Fahy. He assured me that he was on top of things and he would start working on my appeal. I didn't hear back from him. I felt I had been abandoned! Not only did he not submit an appeal on my behalf as he promised, he avoided my calls and never answered any of my written correspondences.

Attorney Nooter stepped back in and filed an appeal on my behalf, but something seemed wrong. While imprisoned I diligently studied the law. Through my studies I learned that Nooter, led by Fahy, failed to properly object to the loss amount in my case. According to Federal Rule 32c(i), all objections must be in writing to the court prior to sentencing. Although my attorney argued for a downward departure based on the actual appraised value of the homes and the "sweet-heart" sale to Lipka, he failed to properly challenge the loss amount on record. This was the key argument that could have significantly reduced my sentence. As a result, I never had a loss hearing to determine the true loss amount in my case. I was surprised that Fahy, nor Nooter caught this blatant error.

In late 2009, I was shipped from prison back to the Bergen County jail to finally address the open case that I had originally retained Fahy to handle. I reached out to Fahy again. It had been 18 months since I'd heard from him. This time, he came to see me at the jail. By the time he made his visit, my former attorney, Paul Casterliero had already worked out a deal with the prosecutor. Fahy advised me that the deal was good and I should take it. I also showed him the errors I found in my New Jersey federal case. At this point my direct appeal was already denied. From this denial, I further learned that my former attorney, Nooter, had misinterpreted the law concerning "materiality" as a defense to bank fraud. He wrongly believed that because the bank's employees didn't rely on the false documentation that was submitted to approve the loans in my case, it was a defense to bank fraud under the "materiality" doctrine. In other words, I went to trial without any viable defense. In addition, just 59 days after I was sentenced, Lehman Brothers Bank collapsed. The bankruptcy findings of the bank revealed that the corporate policies of the bank were premised on fraudulent lending practices and the bank funded over a billion dollars in fraudulent loans. This new evidence supported the fact that I was not the "mastermind" of the scheme as alleged by the bank's attorneys. It had always been my claim that I was instructed by Lehman associates on just what to do to ensure that each loan in question in my case met the bank's underwriting guidelines. I explained all of this to Fahy, who agreed I had several strong arguments for a 2255 ineffective assistance of counsel claim, which could reverse my lengthy sentence. I asked if he would help to prepare this document on my behalf, and he agreed.

After leaving the Bergen County jail in early 2010, I never heard back from Fahy about my case again. Consequently, I was left penniless without funds to retain another attorney, so I had no choice but to prepare my 2255 motion myself.

In June 2011, I initiated a complaint against Fahy with the N.J Fee Arbitration Committee in an attempt to get back the money he had taken. After two years of Fahy repeating his pattern of being nonresponsive, the Fee Arbitration Committee scheduled a hearing for February 21, 2013. My dad, who was my co-litigant on the complaint, appeared in person and I participated via telephone from the Danbury Federal Prison Camp, where I am housed in Connecticut. To my surprise Fahy showed up to the hearing! Fahy told the panel that he never received the first fee arbitration demand that I initiated. And, he said that he didn't respond to the matter because he didn't believe that my dad had standing to file as the "client," even though my father's name was on the fee agreement and he accepted a check directly from him from his retirement account.

The panel did not find good cause to vacate the default as Fahy requested. And, Fahy was openly reprimanded by the committee for not responding to the three letters sent by them on December 6 2011, January 9, 2012, and September 19, 2012. As a result, the panel would not consider any evidence from Fahy. He was only permitted to cross examine me during the hearing.

Through a gruesome cross examination which lasted for almost an hour, Fahy rehashed every wrong doing I had ever done in my entire life. He also questioned the work of my first attorney, Walter Timpone, who Alfred Decotiis also referred me to. He alleged that since other attorneys had been paid retainers and had not performed the services they were retained to do, he should have been able to do the same. To my benefit, the panel didn't buy into his argument or discrediting tactics. They ruled in my favor and ordered Fahy to pay back $44,000 of the retainer within 30 days.

Despite the issuance of the order, Fahy failed to comply. Consequently, on May 21, 2013 Isabel McGinty, Assistant Ethics Counsel for the Office of Attorney Ethics filed a motion to the Supreme Court of New Jersey, Disciplinary Review Board, for the suspension of Fahy's license for noncompliance. On June 20, 2013, the Supreme Court ordered that Fahy had 30 days to pay back $44,000 of the retainer to my father or his license would be suspended.

Still left without the resources needed to retain counsel, I was engaged in a fierce legal fight for my freedom, pro se. On

February 27, 2013, just six days after the N.J Fee Arbitration Committee ruling, the Third Circuit Court of Appeals denied my motion for a certificate of appealability to appeal my 2255 denial. I argued that my sentencing judge, Honorable Jose Linares, improperly denied my 2255 utilizing an incorrect standard of law. To measure ineffective assistance claims the Supreme Court utilizes the two prong Strickland standard. Litigants must show that their attorney made an error, which is the first prong. Second, litigants must show that the error resulted in a wrongful conviction or a lengthier sentence for the litigant. (See Strickland v. Washington , 466 U.S 688 (1984)).

In my 2255 denial, Judge Linares agreed that my attorney, Nooter, had misadvised me of the "materiality" doctrine, which met the first prong of Strickland. But, he stated that the "Petitioner cannot show that the result of her trial would have been different 'but for' this allege deficiency." Therefore, he ruled that I didn't meet the second prong of Strickland. (See Davis v. U.S, Civil Action No. 10-4964 (JLL) Denial p8, Document 19, filed 11/28/11). The problem is the Strickland prejudice standard is not a "but for" standard. It is not outcome determinative. Rather, the standard is whether a reasonable probability exists that, but for the errors, the result would have been different. (See Strickland, 466 U.S. 486, 694 (1984)). Furthermore, the Supreme Court makes it clear in "Lafler," the test is not whether a subsequent trial was otherwise fair and valid, but instead whether the process leading up to the election of trial over plea was constitutionally adequate under Strickland. (See Lafler v. Cooper 182 L.Ed. 2d 398 (2012).

In my case, had I known I was going to trial without ANY viable defense, I would have elected to take a plea. My attorney, Nooter, made a blatant error, which violated my right to effective counsel. It was my constitutional right to have the correct interpretation of the law explained to me, prior to making the choice to go to trial. This can not be disputed! Instead of scheduling an evidentiary hearing, as required by law when a petitioner makes a valid ineffective assistance of counsel claim (which can not be ruled out solely by the record), my judge simply blocked my case from being reopened, and dismissed my case citing an incorrect interpretation of the law. Just to be sure that it was not an oversight on his part, I submitted a motion for reconsideration, again citing the Strickland law, and provided additional case law (ie. Lafler). Once again, the judge denied my motion. This time he erroneously characterized my reconsideration motion as a consecutive 2255, and refused to address the issues in the motion. (See Davis v. U.S, Civil Action No. 10-4964 (JLL) Denial, filed May 30, 2012).

Oddly, the day after my 2255 denial, I also received a final default judgment against me in Lehman's civil case for 34.6 million dollars, which I had been challenging. For several years I fought relentlessly, representing myself, against Chicago Title attorneys, who were headed by Michael R. O'Donnell. Chicago Title was Lehman's insurer who intervened in Lehman's civil case. During my legal research, I had a FOIA request initiated on my behalf to the Office of Comptroller of Currency (OCC) (formerly the Office Of Thrift and Supervision (OTS)). The FOIA request revealed that Lehman's affiliate Aurora Loan Services (the company that originated, processed and underwrote all the loans in my case) did not have authorization from the OTS to originate, underwrite or service loans on behalf of Lehman Brothers FSB (a FDIC bank) in 2002. I submitted this new evidence to both the federal and state court prior to my 2255 ruling. After receiving the denials from both courts, a day apart, refusing to entertain my legitimate arguments or hold an evidentiary hearing, I was lead to believe that something bigger and more powerful was going on, of which I had no clue. Consequently, I believe it was enormous outside power and influence that helped to block my legal arguments on all levels. I knew at this point the only way I could succeed was to take a nontraditional route in my fight for justice. Therefore, I decided to write a book detailing the fraud and corruption that took place in my case, entitled "The High Price I Had To Pay." (See www.smashwords.com/books/view/324608)

On May 15, 2013, I submitted a motion for rehearing to the Third Circuit Court of Appeals. And, under separate cover, I sent a copy of my book along with a letter addressed to Chief Judge Theodore McKee. I also sent this package to the other 23 Third Circuit Court of Appeal Judges. In my letter to the Chief Judge, dated May 17, 2013, I expressed that I felt I was being penalized and discriminated against for being a pro se litigant, and I felt my motion for a mere certificate of appealability was improperly denied. I further explained that I was not a pro se litigant by choice, and I described the difficulties I had with John Jay Fahy. In my letter I also included a copy of the ruling from the N.J. Fee Arbitration Committee. I believed if the judges could see that I had the ability to write about my experiences and expose what I believed to be the deep rooted corruption surrounding my case, they would take my motion seriously. I was wrong!

Unfortunately the Court of Appeals denied my motion for rehearing enbanc. (See U.S v. Davis No. 12-2662, 3rd Cir, Feb 27, 2013). I couldn't help but wonder if Fahy or Judge Linares had been contacted about the letter and the books that I sent to the appeal judges. Had someone reached out to them and questioned the injustices in my case or initiated an inquiry? Or, had my efforts simply fallen on death ears? My goal was to gain back my freedom. I never intended to cause anyone harm.

Involuntarily, it seems like I have become a lead actress in a movie with more twists and turns than the world's fastest roller coaster. Just when I thought things were finally beginning to resolve, I learned of Fahy's death. This leaves many more questions in the air. I have always questioned why Fahy didn't simply help me when he had all the pieces to the puzzle, the "know how" and the experience that could have set me free?

I questioned who the real players were that made off with the money from the property sales in my case? I questioned why my judge blocked all my motions, all along from the beginning to the present, when I had valid arguments? And now, I question why John Jay Fahy killed himself? Why didn't he return the retainer he took for representing me? Was someone applying some kind of unseen pressure to him?

Despite my obstacles, I still believe justice will one day be rendered on my behalf. What I don't know is what price I'll have to pay in order to see it? I obviously don't know what will happen next. But, I do know that none of the events that have occurred in my case over the last several years make logical sense. John Fahy's death adds greatly to this bizarre nightmare that has become my life. My sympathy goes out to his family and friends. I pray one day soon all of our suffering will end.

SUMMARY OF
POST CONVICTION EFFORTS

US v. Jamila Davis
Case # Cr-05-483 (Dist. N.J. 2005)

I. BACKGROUND

A. INITIAL DISTRICT COURT CRIMINAL CASE

I was indicted in June of 2005 on charges of mortgage fraud based on several mortgage applications I assisted in being facilitated, where straw buyers were used to obtain mortgages greater in value than the purchase price of the property, in order to use the surplus for property repair. False documents supported the applications. The case was notable in that 1) the lender's mortgage servicer (Lehman Bros' agent Aurora Lending) encouraged and guided the false application process, and 2) the government impeded my efforts to mitigate loss by obtaining buyers for the properties post-indictment, subsequently selling those properties to a Lehman Bros. insider at a deep discount. I chose to go to trial on these charges because my lawyer misadvised me. He told me that the false applications weren't fraud where the Aurora mortgage officer in fact knew of the false statements and therefore couldn't have relied on them, and that if I wanted to challenge the loss claimed by Lehman, I had to go to trial. Of course, it turned out my lawyer was dead wrong: the false applications were fraud if a reasonable banker would have relied on them, regardless whether Lehman's agent actually did. And, loss calculation was an issue only for sentencing, not for the guilt or innocence determination made at trial. The Honorable

Jose Linares of the US District Court for the District of New Jersey was my judge.

I was convicted by jury verdict on Sept. 20, 2007. I was sentenced on July 16, 2008 to 151 months based on a determination that actual loss was over $14 million (in white collar sentencing, loss amount is the key factor). At my sentencing, my lawyer did not challenge the government's loss estimate, even though we had defense appraisals of the properties that showed by fair market value analysis little or no overall bank loss. Instead, defense counsel only claimed that loss was overstated, and that I should therefore get a downward departure. That meant I had not preserved the core loss issue for appeal.

B. DIRECT APPEAL

My defense counsel handled my direct appeal. The Third Circuit Court of Appeals upheld my conviction on July 1, 2009 (US v. Rickard, 336 Fed. Appx. 235). It rejected the claim that what Aurora in fact relied on was relevant, upholding the lower court's "reasonable lender" standard. The Court stated: "We see no error in the District Court's decision because Petitioner's proposed instruction is not a correct statement of the law." Ibid. It rejected any challenge to my loss calculation because my attorney had not raised it in his opening brief, nor had he preserved the issue at sentencing. The Court stated: "Davis argued for the first time that the total loss resulting from the scheme was incorrectly calculated. Since she did not raise this claim before, we will not consider it." Ibid. Indeed, in my reply brief, my attorney had openly conceded that he made a big mistake not challenging core loss calculation at sentencing: "[I] should have urged the sentencing court to review the calculation of the 'loss amount'... in making the initial guideline calculation of the base offense level, rather than arguing that the loss amount overstated the seriousness of the crime...." March 9, 2009 Reply Brief at p. 15.

II. SECTION 2255 MOTION TO CORRECT/VACATE SENTENCE

On September 28, 2010, I filed a Petition to Vacate, Set Aside or Correct Sentence under 28 USC 2255 (a habeas petition). I raised about 7 issues - that the bank funds weren't FDIC-insured, and that lawyer represented me ineffectively because he misadvised me on materiality, failed to litigate loss, failed to object to restitution, failed to adequately review discovery, failed to interview certain witnesses and experts, and failed to raise a critical appeal issue (loss).

My defense counsel responded by an affidavit attached to the government's answer. He said that it didn't matter what he advised me on materiality because the trial outcome wouldn't have been different. He breezed over the other points, claiming that he did cover loss adequately. The advice issue was key. Under Third Circuit law (US v. Day, 969 F.2d 39 (1992), when a lawyer misadvises his client and causes them to choose trial over a guilty plea, it doesn't matter if the trial is ultimately fair. What matters is that the lawyer's incorrect advice caused the client to choose an option that was harmful to her best interests. Judge Linares ignored this law and denied my 2255 petition. On this issue, he simply adopted the government's response that the trial was ultimately fair so no harm occurred. Judge Linares stated:

Petitioner alleges that her counsel was ineffective because he failed to advise [her] of the correct interpretation of the law of materiality as it relates to a possible defense for bank fraud. However, Petitioner cannot show that the result of her trial would have been different 'but for' this alleged] deficiency. Thus, the prejudice prong of Strickland is not satisfied. Notwithstanding counsel's misapplication of the materiality standard [regarding one set of documents the 2255 claim still fails because those documents were not the only falsified documents at trial. Indeed, [there were] more as no way to argue these were not material. For these reasons important documents the government presented

THE HIGH PRICE I HAD TO PAY

and there w, Petitioner fails the Strickland test. Although [counsel's] approach...may have been deficient...the result would not have been different for Petitioner. This element is dismissed.

Denial of Nov 11, 2011, at pp. 8-9. (Linares also misunderstood the basic "reasonable probability" standard of Strickland. It isn't "but for" the mistake, the result would be different; it's "but for" the mistake, there's a reasonable probability that the result would be different. Strickland v. Washington, 466 US 688, 693 (1986.) Linares also held that defense counsel did not err by failing to raise fair market value loss because it wasn't accepted law.

On December 19, 2011, I filed a Motion to Reconsider the 2255 denial. I presented my facts more cogently in a Supplemental Affidavit, giving great detail as to attorney-client communication, exactly what was said to me and how it caused me to choose trial over pleading guilty. I focused on my lawyer's misadvise on materiality, loss and intent, stating that it doesn't matter if the trial was fair or not; what mattered was that his misadvise caused me to choose an option that was not in my best interests. I also re-raised his failure to litigate loss, showing that the argument he should have made was already well-accepted in the Third Circuit. None of these arguments were new claims.

On March 12, 2012, the Supreme Court issued a decision in Lafler v. Cooper, 566 US ___, 132 S.Ct 1376. There, a defendant also claimed that his lawyer gave wrong legal advice, causing him to choose trial over a guilty plea. The Supreme Court held that the duty to represent a client fairly applies to the plea negotiation process, stating that the fact that a trial may prove fair down the road doesn't fix the problem caused by the lawyer's initial misadvice; the outcome to be worried about is the client's decision, not the trial result. It expressly adopted the Third Circuit's decision in Day, supra. "Far from curing error, the trial causes the injury from the error. Even if the trial is free from constitutional error, the defendant who goes to trial instead of taking a more favorable plea may be prejudiced from either a conviction on more serious counts or the imposition of a more severe sentence." Id., 182 L.Ed. 2d at 409. I immediately brought this case to my judge's attention in a supplemental filing in early April 2012, noting that it was exactly the same point I was raising.

On May 29, 2012, Judge Linares denied my Motion to Reconsider. He said I was not raising any problems in his first denial but instead raising new grounds, making my motion to reconsider akin to a second habeas, which I wasn't authorized to file. Of course, none of that was true. Then he said that, even if he did consider my claims, none of them had merit anyway. He didn't discuss or even acknowledge the Supreme Court's new decision in Lafler.

III. RULE 33 MOTION FOR A NEW TRIAL

I also moved on November 4, 2010 for a new trial based on significant new evidence that appeared after my sentencing. I was referring to Lehman Bros.' bankruptcy filing on September 11, 2008, an act which propelled the world economy to the point of collapse. Its bankruptcy was based on years of predatory mortgage lending where Lehman and its agent, Aurora Lending, deliberately solicited and approved ill-qualified Alt-A loans, then commercialized this worthless paper. Scores of congressional and academic reports after the debacle identified these practices as the core factor underlying the 2008 global financial collapse. I presented some of these reports to Judge Linares, to show that Lehman's nationwide fraud practices were the same as what had occurred in my case: the Aurora loan officer solicited and approved false mortgage applications for our Alt-A loans. I thought this should impact guilt or innocence, or at least the scope of the punishment, in my case, for how could a bank be a victim of its own fraudulent practices?

On October 20, 2011, Judge Linares again denied me relief. He made the ludicrous statement that, if only I had dug more deeply, I would have discovered these nationwide Lehman practices and been able to raise them at my trial.

"Despite the fact that the [submitted] articles [setting forth the full scope of Lehman's global fraud] were not written until after [Davis] was convicted, the substance of them as it relates to...certain...loans were known by [her] at trial. Indeed, [Davis' counsel] 'attempted to prove' that Aurora...'participated in the fraud' but simply 'did not have access to the [Lehman] information...until after it collapsed.... [Davis], however had over 18 months between the initial indictment and the start of the trial to perform [her] due diligence. Although it is debatable whether reasonable diligence could have unearthed the evidence now presented within the 18 month time-frame, [Davis] was free to ask the Court for more time if needed.

Rule 33 Denial, Oct 21, 2011, pp 4-5. Therefore, the bankruptcy and scope of practices information did not qualify as "new evidence." Nor, the court stated, were the loans in my case the same type as those in Lehman's bankruptcy - a clearly wrong statement of fact. Linares said my loans were subprime, when in fact all of the loans in my case were Alt-A loans, so-called "liar loans, the same type as most of those involved in the Lehman collapse. See testimony of Lehman representative Carl Peterson, Sept. 10, 2007, Trial Transcript pp. 4.134, 4.48, 5.37. 5/43. 4.48.

I also moved for reconsideration here, too, showing the record evidence that the loans were the same type and pointed out the absurdity of the belief that one defendant in a single case could have uncovered the full scope of Lehman's global practices, a scope which took sophisticated academics and other professionals years to unearth. It was a ridiculous conclusion. Predictably, Judge Linares denied this motion jointly with his denial of my 2255 reconsideration motion.

IV. APPELLATE REVIEW

In July 2012 I appealed both these denials to the Third Circuit Court of Appeals. As to the 2255, I pointed out the direct contraction between Judge Linares' position on legal misadvise - that it is irrelevant because the trial outcome was ultimately fair - and the Supreme Court's very clear statement in Lafler v. Cooper that whether the trial is fair or not does not matter because the damage from the legal misadvise is that it causes the defendant to choose trial over plea and put himself at greater risk for a longer sentence. I also showed that whether a loss figure represents fair market value (the issue my lawyer and Linares said was a new test unaccepted in this Circuit) is exactly the test the federal courts (including the Third Circuit) had been using for years to determine actual loss in my circumstances. It was crazy for an experienced defense counsel not to know this law. And counsel had openly admitted he goofed on this point in his direct appeal reply brief. The standard for granting me permission to fully brief is "could reasonable jurists have disagreed" with the lower court's denial, a very low standard. Nonetheless, the Third Circuit denied me permission to fully brief these issues, stating that "no reasonable jurist could have disagreed" with Judge Linares. It was an astounding conclusion, especially given the Supreme Court's decision in Lafler, which so clearly applied to my situation. I then asked the entire bank of Third Circuit judges to look again at this denial; they denied that request, too. In September 2013, I sought Supreme Court review, showing the straightforward conflict between the denials to date and their own recent decision in Lafler. The Supreme Court denied me permission to appeal, and my habeas came to an end.

I also sought Third Circuit review of the lower court's denial of my Rule 33 new trial motion, where Judge Linares claimed I could have discovered Lehman's massive fraud myself had I been more diligent. Unbelievably, the entire Third Circuit bench found no error here, either. They rejected the idea that a financial institution riddled with fraudulent management practices could not itself be a victim of those same practices. I raised this last issue before the Supreme Court, and they rejected it, too. Thus my criminal conviction became final.

VICTIMS OF MASS INCARCERATION: THE NEW JIM CROW FOR WOMEN

Written by: Jamila T. Davis

After reading a newly published Fact Sheet about Mass Incarceration, on the top bunk in my 5 1/2 x 9 cubicle in federal prison, I had a revelation that startled me for a moment. Even though I've been called every name in the book by my prosecutor, former U.S. Attorney Christopher Christie, and labeled as the 25 year old "mastermind" who deserved to serve a decade plus sentence behind bars, the truth is I am a victim. Like many others trapped in prisons across this country, I am a victim of mass incarceration.

First hand, I have witnessed what I believe to be the root cause of mass incarceration, Over-Sentencing. In 2008, I was sentenced to 12 1/2 years for bank fraud, as a real estate investor. My alleged victim was the now-defunct Lehman Brothers Bank. Just 59 days after I was sentenced, the bank collapsed and the world discovered the rampant, fraudulent mortgage lending practices of the bank. After the evidence surfaced, it was proven that Lehman was not a victim at all, rather a mass-victimizer, yet I remain trapped behind bars. Even worst, I am not alone in suffering injustices.

The U.S. leads the world with the largest prison population. Even though the U.S. population consists of only 5% of the world's population, it holds 25% of the world's prison population. Currently, there are over 2 million Americans behind bars, and the numbers continue to steadily grow. From 1970 to present, the prison population has increased seven fold! Consequently, a quarter of the nation's adult population has a criminal record, and our country spends a quarter of a trillion dollars each year on criminal justice. Do the statistics correctly portray Americans to the world as the most dangerous country, filled with heathens who commit far more serious crimes than any other nation? Could this really be true? Or, is there another explanation for our country's mass incarceration epidemic?

History paints a clear picture of how our country got enthralled into mass incarceration. In 1987 the Sentencing Reform Act of 1984 (SRA) was enacted as a part of the War on Drugs. With this new legislation, stricter laws and penalties were enforced by the federal government, and most states followed suite. Prior to these changes, the maximum term of imprisonment for the possession of any drug, in any amount, in the U.S. judicial system was one year, which is consistent with the sentencing norms in many countries today. After 1987 that penalty was increased drastically from one year to life in prison without the possibility of parole. Not only did the new laws effect drug offenders, they increased punishment for all federal offenders, eliminating federal parole and decreasing good time allowances. Additionally, the U.S. Sentencing Guidelines were also enacted in 1987 mandating judges to sentence all defendants in accordance to the new harsher sentencing scales. Consequently, the number of prisoners behind bars skyrocketed!

The goal of the War on Drugs initiative was to decrease crime, yet the public now knows it was dreadfully unsuccessful. More disheartening, it was destructive! Thousands were imprisoned for significant periods of time, serving no constructive purpose. Consequently, the population of federal prisoners grew from approximately 24,000 inmates in 1980 to roughly 220,000 inmates today. Out of this large population, only 5% of federal prisoners are violent offenders. The rest are non-violent offenders, of which many are serving lengthy sentences. As a direct result of mass incarceration, the Bureau of Prisons (BOP), the entity that houses federal prisoners, is currently 40% over capacity. And, no viable solution has been proposed to combat this serious issue. Instead of addressing the root problem - defective sentencing legislation - this problem still remains unaddressed!

There is a smart, cost effective, solution to address the issue of over mass incarceration within the U.S. federal prison system that can be enacted rather quickly. The government can easily revert back to the old pre-1987 laws; reinstating federal parole and increasing good time allowances. This would restore families and save tax payers billions of dollars. It would seem like this is the most logical simple solution, so why haven't measures been taken to correct this vital issue? Who is holding up the process? And, who stands to benefit most from the prison sector that is currently in place? The answers to those questions would explain why our country's mass incarceration epidemic still exits.

Most people could care less about mass incarceration, because they feel it doesn't personally effect them. Therefore, the American people have not made a demand for change. Six years ago I didn't believe it would personally affect me either, but today I am a victim of the wrath. Behind bars, I am surrounded by a slew of professionals, including former doctors, lawyers and politicians that also never thought they'd be victims of the fiery reigns of mass incarceration. Who's next?

As times have changed, so has the U.S. prison population. More and more women are behind bars in America. According to the Bureau of Justice, in a 20 year span the rate of incarceration for women has increased 800%. Women are no longer exempt from prosecution. More vulnerable and willing to except a plea deal versus trial, females have become easy targets of mass incarceration. Consequently, families across our nation are being destroyed, with nearly 3 million children (most under the age of 10) with a parent in prison.

Confined behind bars, there is little we can do as prisoners, but as a free citizen you can create change! Therefore, I would urge all Americans to take a second look at this cruel epidemic that has proven to destroy families and demoralize our country. When you see the faces and the backgrounds of many of us serving lengthy sentences for nonviolent crimes, including tax evasion, you will most likely be shocked! The check of one wrong box on an application can lead anyone to prison, no matter how old you are, and even if it is your first offense. Please view the slide show at www.WomenOverIncarcerated.org to gain a greater visual of who is serving time behind bars.

After viewing this slide, and re-examining the facts, please answer this question: Do you feel the sentences that were handed down to me, and the women in the slide, represent justice? Then, decide, if you believe we are victims of mass incarceration? Your opinion certainly counts! Without you, we have no voice!

Did you know that ALL federal offenders must serve a little over 85% of their sentences (with good time credit) because of the absence of federal parole? Consequently, federal offenders often serve double, or in some cases more than triple, the time of state offenders who commit the same or similar crimes. Please help to level the scales of justice by supporting the WomenOverIncarcerated prison reform movement. Go to www.womenoverincarcerated.org and sign the online petition today. Your support can make a difference. Please, SPEAK OUT!

Poems For Incarcerated Women

Written By: Jamila T. Davis

"With my pen I love to scribe love letters to those who are suffering and can use a word of encouragement. I can relate because I personally know their struggles and their pain. Poetry is the tool I use to share my testimony, with hope that others will learn from my experiences."

Will You Give Me Another Chance?

Written By: Jamila T. Davis

Dear Sir or Ma'am,

To you I may be that numbered file that's stacked high on your desk
That represents the wrong I've done, in the midst of all my mess.
Yes, I've done my share of things that don't make me very proud,
Trying to be a "people-pleaser," moving with the wrong crowd!
And I know you probably view me as a villain or a crook;
But I ask you not to judge me by the cover of the book.
I do have a name and an identity. I have a story to tell!
There's a reason behind the story why I landed up in jail.
And no, I'm not getting ready to give you a lame excuse.
But I got to tell you, I've been through a lot! I've suffered so much abuse!
All I ever wanted was to be accepted; to be loved.
Instead, this life done beat me down. I've been pushed, and I've been shoved!
This story I tell, it started from the very day of my birth.
Life for me ain't been no crystal stair, since I came into this Earth!
So many disappointments! So much hurt, and so much shame.
That led me down this criminal path I thought would ease my pain.
The more I tried to escape, the bigger the hole I dug.
If I could have only found that one who'd stop and show me love!

Could you imagine what it's like from youth to be told that you
*   would fail?*
"Little girl, you'll never be nothing, you gonna end up right in jail!"
And I believed them when they said, "You're a liar and you're
*   a cheat!"*
And guess what? I became those very words that led to my defeat!
Then I stood before you, listening to words I recognized.
The way that you described me, am I garbage in your eyes?
Hey, I don't want to be that person you talked about in your speech!
I've got goals and I have dreams that I need your help to reach!
Yeah, I know it's easy to lock me up, and throw away the key.
But what about you stopping and helping me become a better me?
Don't just give me a place to sit, give me the resources I need to
*   change.*
And please don't place them far away; make sure they're within
*   my range!*
Have you ever messed up? Have you ever made a mistake?
Has life been always peaches and cream or like a piece of cake?
Was there ever someone special who offered you a hand?
And if so, what effects did it have in your becoming a woman
*   or a man?*
All I'm really looking for is a chance to become my greater self!
I know I can do it with the right tools and a little of your help.
Do you know how very much your encouraging words would mean?
They could change my entire life and make a difference that
*   can be seen!*
Please don't give up on me; I promise I'll do my best!
Don't lock me up and throw me away, like they do to all the rest!
I'm sorry! I didn't mean it! I really want to change!
I was wrong! I make no excuse! I accept the blame!
Please view me as you should, as someone whose life you can
*   enhance.*
Please oh please, Mr. Sir or Ma'am,
Will you give me another chance?

I Surrender –
A Prisoner's Cry

By Jamila T. Davis

There comes a point in our lives when enough becomes enough!
When constant troubles arise, and life is way too rough.
Like a bomb that drops, all hell breaks loose, without a person
*   in sight to give us a boost.*
All our poor judgments backfire in our face, and those who we
*   trusted become informants in our case.*
Everything we try begins to quickly fail, surrounded by these
*   cinder blocks, in our new home we call jail.*
On our bunks we stop and think, "How in the world did we land
*   here?" That's when our problems come to light, causing*
*   pain too great to bear.*
Some of us started off as that sweet innocent child.
She had two ponytails, big fat cheeks and an irresistible smile.
One day she was lured by someone she thought she could
*   trust,*
Who snatched away her youth as his hands fondled her bust.
The shame never left, the reproach settled in.
Next thing she knows she's caught up in a lifestyle of sin.
Then there're those of us who started off fine, who lived in a nice
*   house, whose parents were kind.*
Things were great, she's headed for success! Then she met her
*   love, that's when her life turned into a mess.*
Blinded by love, she couldn't see, had no clue this kind of love
*   would ruin her destiny.*

Then there's one who struggled from the day of her birth,
With daddy in jail and momma on crack, since she entered this place called "Earth."
There were many nights the cupboard was bare, she had no food to eat.
In a quest to survive she sought love, now she rocks designer shoes on her feet.
Her love had the money rolling in, but as a drug dealer's girl, her new problems begin.
When the troubles came many of us tried to escape, looking for the solutions to bypass the yellow tape.
She started with weed and it put her at ease.
But one day she discovered the weed would no longer please.
Then she tried coke, then crack, then dope.
When that didn't work she lost her hope.
Whatever it was we were all sold out!
For a moment no struggles, no worries, no doubts.
Then like a whirlwind, the storms began to come:
The things we did we thought were wise, turned out to be so dumb.
In the storm we learned so much, no longer blind to life.
We learned that love wasn't love at all when it stabbed us like a knife.
Where are all our friends who were around when everything was up?
They're out seeking a free ride; who'll be next to fill their cup?
Things aren't what they seem to be. What we thought was an escape, became a tragedy.
We found out in the end we only have our self.
Some of us are left beat down and robbed, HIV done stole our health.
Bad choices and poor decisions led us to this very place. And on top of all that misery, now we got this case.
There's got to be another way. Things can't stay like this! Left inside this lonely place, our families greatly missed.

Pushed so hard against the walls, depression has us bound.
It is not until we get to this place that true help can be found.
Are you tired of running in circles?
Are you tired of the hurt and pain?
Are you finally convinced you must surrender because life will
never change?
What about the kids you left behind?
Is it fair to them, that they, too, must do this time?
What about the others who hurt because of our pain? Will you
change for them or will you stay the same?
It's time to make a choice; is enough, enough?
Are you ready to release the shackles and take off the handcuffs?
Are you ready for a brand new life? Where you can be a mother,
a friend and a wife!
Are you ready to achieve your dreams, without having to watch
your back? When life can finally be filled with plenty and we
no longer suffer lack!
You can have it, it's your choice! You can sign the agreement
with your voice!
I surrender, I surrender, is all you have to say. That's when help
will come your way.
Are you ready to follow me now, down this road called change?
I promise, if you surrender today, your life won't be the
same.
Open your mouth and throw up your hands.
With your voice release the shackles and bands.
There's nothing left but for us to say, "I give up this old life, I
surrender today!"

Permission To Dream

By Jamila T. Davis

Young lady, pick up your head and dry your teary eyes.
You don't have to stay stuck in a ditch; it's time for you to arise!
The past is done, so let it go.
A painful lesson, but now you know.
Everything that happened occurred for a reason.
The pain that you bear will only last for a season.
Never ever think it was all for nothing.
This storm has a rainbow; it will surely count for something!
It wasn't sent to hurt you or to even beat you down.
It's heaven's way of saying, "It's time to turn your life around."
Now that you're here, at this place, you're finally ready to soar!
Greatness lies just ahead, right behind the prison doors.
You're standing at the crossroads, divided by your choice;
You can take back what was stolen, by your imagination and
*   your voice.*
Revisit your days of youth, life as that little girl,
Who could become whatever she wanted or dreamed of in this
*   world.*
Take hold of all the dreams you had from way back then.
Embrace them like a treasure; treat them like your closest
*   friend.*
It's time to regroup, so that you can begin again.
Trust me; it won't be like before, this time you're sure to win!
Rise up and discard all the shame, regret and guilt.
On high self-esteem, this new house must be built.
You made some mistakes, but yet you're still a shining star!

Has anyone told you lately, how truly wonderful you are?
You're a special person. Yes, you're one of a kind!
God put you on this earth, for sure, to let your bright light shine!
Everything will come together, when you discover your purpose.
There's so much more to you than what appears upon the surface.
It's time to dig deep, and do some rearranging down inside.
It's time to show off your talents; you no longer have to hide.
Yesterday doesn't determine the state of your fate.
You can rise above adversity; it's never ever too late!
You can become whatever you desire;
And when you reach that goal, you still can go higher.
You no longer have to be afraid of what others think or what they say.
Young lady, it's your time to shine. Today marks a brand new day!
Give back all the baggage you've been given to hold you down.
Dust off your defilement; begin to turn your life around.
Stop regretting all the things you never got to do.
Instead do something about it, and experience something new!
Spread your wings and begin to fly!
Peel away your past, tell yesterday goodbye.
Yes, you can do it! Let your bright light beam!
Today I formally give you back your permission to dream.

My Daughter

Written by: Jamila T. Davis

*My daughter when I look down from heaven and I notice you,
you bring a smile to My face.*
*I know you think your life is off track, but you're surely in the
right place.*
*I've listened to you intently, when you've cried out for My
help.*
*And I realized that you don't understand the cards that you've
been dealt.*

No it's not a curse, a mishap, or a scam.
Everything that happened to you was written in My plan.
*From the day that you asked Me, I quickly answered your
prayers.*
*But you rejected My solutions, that's why you shed so many
tears.*

Yes I know My daughter you desire joy and you want peace.
And I know you just can't wait for all your obstacles to cease.
*But My daughter don't you know, if there is no pain, there is no
gain?*
*So when I'm molding you for greatness, why do you tend to
complain?*

*Don't you know how much I love you, My wonderful, precious
child?*
When I look down from Heaven you make Me so very proud!

When you feel lost inside, it's Me saying, "I'll guide you through this day."
So why don't you trust and depend on Me, and let Me lead the way?

Why do you think you have all the answers? Do you really know what's best?
Instead of enduring through obstacles, you try hard to avoid My tests.
The quicker you surrender, the quicker you'll get through.
And when this storm is over, your life will be brand new!

You can trust Me, My daughter. I have you in the palm of My hand.
What I have for you is better that what you can get from any man!
Let go of all your crutches, and rid yourself of shame and guilt.
You are stronger than you think, for you are the creation that I built!

There is purpose behind your pain, and a reason for every tear you shed.
The more that you cried out to Me, the more your spirit I fed.
In this fiery furnace, I'll mold you to become your best.
How would you know what you're made of, without My trials and My tests?

Everything you thought you needed is planted deep inside.
Because within your spirit is the place where I reside.
My daughter, be of good courage. This season too shall pass.
Whatever you need is a prayer away, all you have to do is ask.

Never ever forget I am here for you. You can reach out any time.
I just wanted to let you know I love you, and I'm glad that you are Mine.

So dry your tears My daughter, and hold your head up high.
This is just a little reminder, you're the apple of My eye!

About the Author

J amila T. Davis, born and raised in Jamaica Queens, New York, is a motivational speaker and the creator of the Voices of Consequences Enrichment Series for incarcerated women. Through her powerful delivery, Davis illustrates the real-life lessons and consequences that result from poor choices. She also provides the techniques and strategies that she  personally has utilized to dethrone negative thinking patterns, achieve emotional healing, and restoration and growth.

Davis is no stranger to triumphs and defeats. By the age of 25, she utilized her business savvy and street smarts to rise to the top of her field, becoming a lead go-to-person in the Hip-Hop Music Industry and a self-made millionaire through real estate investments. Davis lived a care-free lavish lifestyle, surrounded by rap stars, professional sports figures and other well known celebrities.

All seemed well until the thorn of materialism clouded Davis' judgments and her business shortcuts backfired, causing her self-made empire to crumble. Davis was convicted of bank fraud, for her role in a multi-million dollar bank fraud scheme, and sentenced to 12 1/2 years in federal prison.

Davis' life was in a great shambles as she faced the obstacle of imprisonment. While living in a prison cell, stripped of all her worldly possessions, and abandoned by most of her peers, she was forced to deal with the root of her dilemmas- her own inner self.

Davis searched passionately for answers and strategies to heal and regain her self-confidence, and to discover her life's purpose. She utilized her formal training from Lincoln University, in Philadelphia, Pennsylvania, along with her real-life post-incarceration experiences and documented her discoveries. Revealing the tools, techniques and strategies she used to heal, Davis composed a series of books geared to empower women. Davis' goal is to utilize her life experiences to uplift, inspire and empower her audience to achieve spiritual and emotional wholeness and become their very best, despite their dilemmas and past obstacles.

For FREE access to Court or Discovery Documents related to Jamila T. Davis' case, or for more information regarding her case, contact:

Jose Francisco
Francisco & Associates
9100 South Dadeland Blvd.
Suite 1500
Miami, FL 33156
(305)242-0770

For more information about Jamila T. Davis and her books, please visit www.vocseries.com or contact us at:

Voices International Publications Inc.
196-03 Linden Blvd.
St. Albans, NY 11412
(718) 341-1983

OR

You can write Jamila T. Davis directly at the address below:

Jamila T. Davis #59253-053
Danbury Federal Prison Camp
33 1/2 Pembroke Rd
Danbury, CT 06811

Voices International Publications Presents

ᗺoices of
CONSEQUENCES
ENRICHMENT SERIES
CREATED BY: JAMILA T. DAVIS

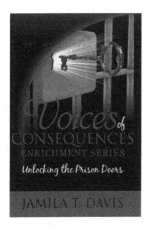

Unlocking the Prison Doors:
12 Points to Inner Healing and
Restoration

ISBN: 978-09855807-4-2 Textbook
ISBN: 978-09855807-5-9 Workbook/Journal
ISBN: 978-09855807-6-6 Curriculum Guide
is a nondenominational, faith-based instructional manual created to help incarcerated women gain inner healing and restoration. In a comforting voice that readers can recognize and understand, this book provides the tools women need to get past the stage of denial and honestly assess their past behavioral patterns, their criminal conduct and its impact on their lives and others. It provides a platform for women to begin a journey of self-discovery, allowing them to assess the root of their problems and dilemmas and learn how to overcome them.

This book reveals real-life examples and concrete strategies that inspire women to release anger, fear, shame and guilt and embrace a new world of opportunities.

After reading readers will be empowered to release the inner shackles and chains that have been holding them bound and begin to soar in life!

INTERNATIONAL PUBLICATIONS
"Changing Lives One Page At A Time."
www.vocseries.com

Voices International Publications Presents

$\mathcal{V}oices$ of
CONSEQUENCES
ENRICHMENT SERIES
CREATED BY: JAMILA T. DAVIS

Permission to Dream:
12 Points to Discovering Your Life's
Purpose and Recapturing Your Dreams

ISBN: 978-09855807-4-2 Textbook
ISBN: 978-09855807-5-9 Workbook/Journal
ISBN: 978-09855807-6-6 Curriculum Guide
is a nondenominational, faith-based, instruction manual created to inspire incarcerated women to discover their purpose in life and recapture their dreams. In a way readers can identify with and understand, this book provides strategies they can use to overcome the stigma and barriers of being an ex-felon.

This book reveals universal laws and proven self-help techniques that successful people apply in their everyday lives. It helps readers identify and destroy bad habits and criminal thinking patterns, enabling them to erase the defilement of their past.

Step-by-step this book empowers readers to recognize their talents and special skill sets, propelling them to tap into the power of "self" and discover their true potential, and recapture their dreams.

After reading , readers will be equipped with courage and tenacity to take hold of their dreams and become their very best!

INTERNATIONAL PUBLICATIONS
"Changing Lives One Page At A Time."
www.vocseries.com

Voices International Publications Presents

$\mathcal{V}oices$ of
CONSEQUENCES
ENRICHMENT SERIES
CREATED BY: JAMILA T. DAVIS

Pursuit to A Greater "Self:" 12 Points to Developing Good Character and HealthyRelationships

ISBN: 978-09855807-7-3 Textbook
ISBN: 978-09855807-8-0 Workbook/Journal
ISBN: 978-09855807-9-7 Curriculum Guide
is a non-denominational, faith-based, instruction manual created to help incarcerated women develop good character traits and cultivate healthy relationships.

This book is filled with real-life examples that illustrate how good character traits have helped many people live a more prosperous life, and how deficient character has caused others to fail. These striking examples, along with self-help strategies revealed in this book, are sure to inspire women to dethrone bad character traits and develop inner love, joy, peace, patience, kindness, generosity, faithfulness, gentleness and self-control. This book also instructs women how to utilize these positive character traits to cultivate healthy relationships.

After reading readers will be inspired to let their light shine for the world to see that true reformation is attainable, even after imprisonment!

VOICES
INTERNATIONAL PUBLICATIONS
"Changing Lives One Page At A Time."
www.vocseries.com

"Every negative choice we make in life comes with a consequence. Sometimes the costs we are forced to pay are severe!"
— Jamila T. Davis

She's All Caught Up is a real-life cautionary tale that exemplifies the powerful negative influences that affect today's youth and the consequences that arise from poor choices.

Young Jamila grew up in a loving middle class home, raised by two hardworking parents, the Davises, in the suburbs of Jamaica Queens, New York. Determined to afford their children the luxuries that they themselves never had, the Davises provided their children with a good life, hoping to guarantee their children's success.

At first it seemed as though their formula worked. Young Jamila maintained straight As and became her parents ideal "star child," as she graced the stage of Lincoln Center's Avery Fischer Hall in dance recitals and toured the country in a leading role in an off-Broadway play. All was copacetic in the Davis household until high school years when Jamila met her first love Craig- a 16 year old drug dealer from the Southside housing projects of Jamaica Queens.

As this high school teen rebels, breaking loose from her parents' tight reins, the Davises wage an "all-out" battle to save their only daughter whom they love so desperately. But Jamila is in too deep! Poisoned by the thorn of materialism, she lusts after independence, power and notoriety, and she chooses life in the fast lane to claim them.

When this good girl goes bad, it seems there is no turning back! Follow author, Jamila T. Davis (creator of the Voices of Consequences Enrichment Series) in her trailblazing memoir, *She's All Caught Up!*

DECEMBER 2013
ISBN: 978-09855807-3-5
www.voicesbooks.com

"Is it fair that corporate giants get to blame 'small fries' like myself, whom they recruited but they walk away scott-free?"
— Jamila T. Davis

Years before the 2008 Financial Crisis, a major epidemic of mortgage fraud surged throughout the country. The FBI geared up to combat the problem, imprisoning thousands who were alleged to have victimized Wall Street giants, such as Lehman Brothers Bank. Hidden safely behind the auspices of being a "victim," savvy Ivy League bank executives created additional fraudulent schemes to further their profit. Utilizing their "victimizers" as scapegoats, the bankers' clever plan went undetected. Consequently, the real architects of the massive fraudulent lending schemes escaped unpunished. And the "small fries," who the bankers blamed to be the bandits, were left to do big time!

The High Price I Had To Pay is a captivating real-life story that reveals another aspect of the inside fraud perpetrated by Lehman executives that has yet to be told!

This illuminating synopsis by author Jamila T. Davis, who is currently serving a 12 1/2 year sentence in federal prison for bank fraud, is shared from a unique stand point. Davis was labeled by Lehman attorneys as the 25 year old mastermind who devised an elaborate mortgage scheme that defrauded their bank of 22 million dollars. Her shocking story captures the inside tricks of Wall Street elite and takes you up-close and personal into a world driven by greed and power.

Davis' story will leave you amazed and make you think. Have savvy Wall Street executives, such as Richard Fuld, been able to out smart the world? And while these executives escape unpunished, is it fair that "small fries," like Davis, are left to do big time?

"I am a 73 Year Old woman currently serving an 11 year sentence in federal prison. One bad decision landed me a decade plus sentence as a first time, non-violent offender."
— Gwendolyn Hemphill

Since 1970, the U.S. prison population has increased seven fold, growing to over 2 million prisoners. Consequently, even though it only consists of 5% of the world's population, America leads the world with the largest prison population. Crime rates are not increasing, yet the U.S. prison population continues to steadily grow. As a result, mass incarceration is a major epidemic that destroys families and costs tax payers billions of dollars each year. The statistics are well known, but the true faces of those imprisoned and the injustices they encounter in the U.S. judicial system is less publicized.

The High Price I Had To Pay, Volume 3, is a captivating true story about the life of Gwendolyn Hemphill, a 73 year old woman currently serving a 11 year sentence for her role in a scheme to defraud the Washington Teachers Union (WTU).

Rising from humble beginnings in the rural town of Johnstown, Pennsylvania, Hemphill worked relentlessly to overcome barriers of poverty and racism. Known for her savvy wit and creative political strategies, she successfully advocated for unions and political groups, including the legendary SNCC, during the era of the civil rights movement. Climbing to the top of the political ladder, as a rising star, Hemphill made her way up to the White House under the Carter Administration. For decades, she vigorously served as a liaison who provided substantial contributions to her community; making waves in the world of Washington D.C. politics. Despite her accomplishments and her stellar career, one bad decision landed Hemphill a decade plus sentence in federal prison, as a first time, non-violent offender.

Hemphill's story gives readers and inside view of the many female, white collar offenders, who are serving lengthy sentences behind bars. This story will leave you questioning is there mercy and equality for all citizens in the U.S. judicial system? And, it will make you think: Should a senior citizen with a stellar past serve a decade plus sentence as a first time, non-violent offender?

NOW AVAILABLE FROM
VOICES
INTERNATIONAL PUBLICATIONS

"This guide is filled with all the valuable information which would have been great to have known prior to my incarceration."
— Lisa Barrett

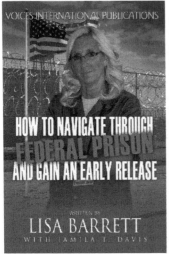

Have you or a loved one been sentenced to serve time in federal prison and have no clue what to expect? The experience doesn't have to be as scary or stressful as you may think. There is a way to overcome this obstacle as quickly as possible and come out on top! Let Lisa Barrett teach you the ropes!

Barrett, a former school teacher and Teacher's Union President sentenced to serve a year in federal prison, utilized her time behind bars to create an invaluable road-map for prisoners. Through her first hand experience, research and interviews with numerous inmates, Barrett has compiled a unique resource for federal prisoners; the first of its kind written from a women's prospective.

How To Navigate Through Federal Prison And Gain An Early Release is a detailed prisoner's survival guide, written by former inmate Lisa Barrett with excerpts by inmate Jamila T. Davis. This captivating book vividly guides readers through the journey of incarceration, shattering the fear of the unknown!

Designed in an easy-to-read format, step-by-step, readers are provided a crash course on the "do's" and "don'ts" for new prisoners, while being enlightened to the scope of services, programs and policies of the Bureau of Prisons (BOP).

From learning what to bring, what you'll need to buy, how to stay connected with the outside world, how to receive money, how to survive on prison food, how to land a decent job, how to utilize your time productively, and much more, Barrett provides a plethora of resources and techniques that are useful to prisoners.

Additionally, this book includes detailed excerpts by inmate/activist Jamila T. Davis on viable legal remedies, strategies to gain relief from the U.S. Courts and BOP available options for early release. Davis, author of *the Voices Of Consequences Enrichment Series* and co-founder of WomenOverIncarcerated.org, shares her 6 1/2 years of hands on experience successfully challenging injustice from behind bars.

Armed with this arsenal of valuable information both male and female readers are sure to be equipped to navigate through federal prison and gain an early release!

FEBRUARY 2015
ISBN:978-0-9911041-4-7
www.voicesbooks.com

NOW AVAILABLE FROM
VOICES 💬
INTERNATIONAL PUBLICATIONS

"Step-by-step, through each commandment, I will teach you how to take adversity and turn it into the launching pad for your success!"
— Sunshine Smith-Williams

Some foolishly believe life is a matter of choice, based on the cards they are dealt. Yet, a Boss Chick knows she can reign as captain of her own ship, regardless of how steep the tides may come! Because life in fact is a matter of choice, a Boss Chick chooses to strategically call the shots and she plays to win! Although she may face challenges at sea, a Boss Chick never travels without her navigation. As a result, when others around her falter, she always seem to have the answers to get ahead, turn around her situations and come out on top!

The key to a Boss Chick's success resonates by the standards she sets and rules she lives by, which keep her rooted and grounded, and give her wisdom to turn adversity into triumph. Everything she needs to know to become a virtuous woman, discover her purpose, find a mate, keep him, gain notoriety and wealth are now outlined in *Sunny 101: The 10 Commandments Of A Boss Chick*, a must-have empowerment guide for today's striving women!

This self-help companion is a road-map designed to empower women to avoid the common pitfalls that often derail many from achieving their dreams. Author Sunshine Smith-Williams enlightens readers how to overcome life obstacles and utilize challenges as fuel for success. Not only does she instruct readers on what to do, through captivating, real-life examples she teaches her readers how to strengthen their endurance, sharpen their insight and reign as an ultimate Boss Chick!

Step-by-step through each poignant Commandment, Smith-Williams equips her readers to overcome fear, increase their self-esteem, build powerful relationships and rise as a shinning star amongst the pack. By implementing a lifestyle, based on morals, values and principles, and setting practical goals, readers are challenged to step up their game, raise the bar on their expectations, and finally live the life of their dreams!

Some believe no woman can have it all, but Smith-Williams enlightens her readers how to beat the odds! No matter what obstacles they may face in life, regardless of background, color or creed, girded with *Sunny 101: The 10 Commandments Of A Boss Chick*, any woman can position herself to come out on top!

Through her candid voice of reason, broken down into easy-to-read revelations, practical analysis and jewel drops, which are sure to stir the soul and stimulate the mind, let Sunshine Smith-Williams teach you the ropes, and you too can become a Boss Chick!

MARCH 2015

ISBN: 978-0-9911041-6-1
www.voicesbooks.com

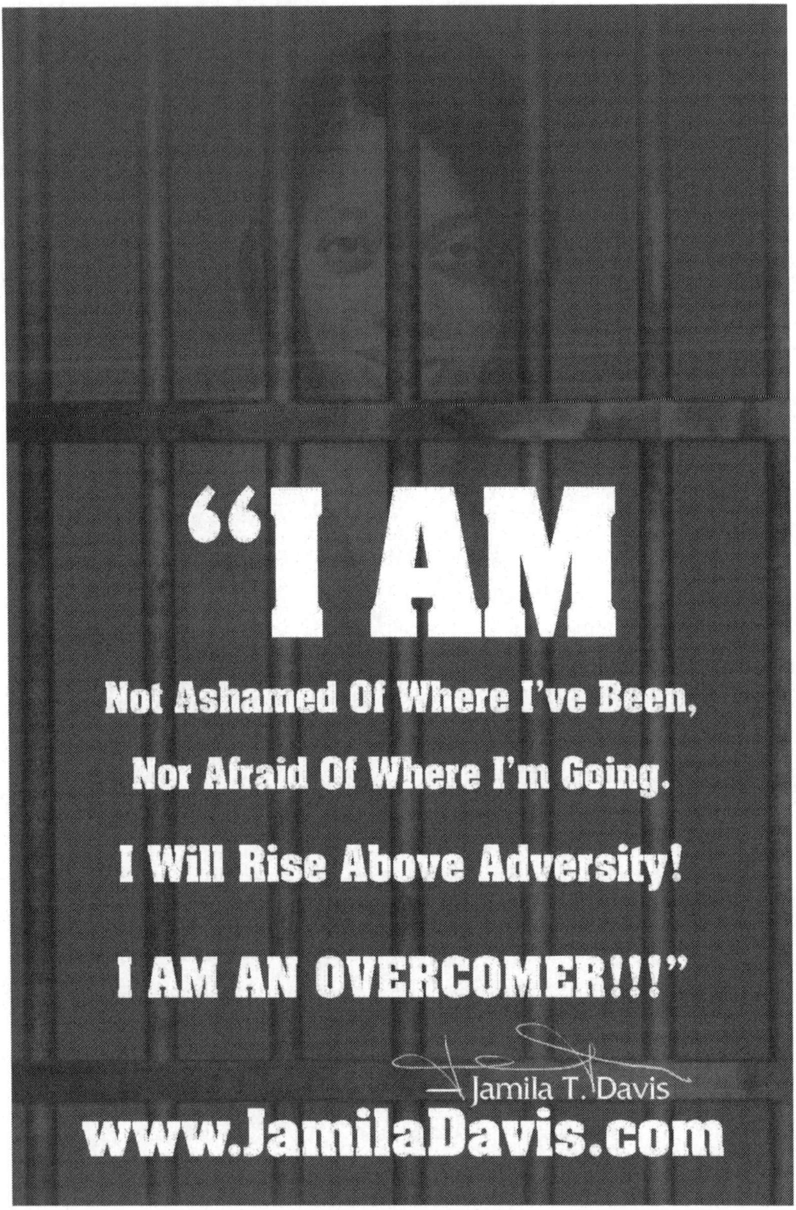
"I AM
Not Ashamed Of Where I've Been,
Nor Afraid Of Where I'm Going.
I Will Rise Above Adversity!
I AM AN OVERCOMER!!!"
Jamila T. Davis
www.JamilaDavis.com

INTERNATIONAL PUBLICATIONS

ORDER FORM

Mail to: 196-03 Linden Blvd.
St. Albans, NY 11412
or visit us on the web @
www.vocseries.com

QTY	Title	Price
	Unlocking the Prison Doors	14.95
	Permission to Dream	14.95
	Pursuit to A Greater "Self"	14.95
	The High Price I Had To Pay 1	7.99
	The High Price I Had To Pay 2	7.99
	The High Price I Had To Pay 3	9.99
	She's All Caught Up- 15.00	15.00
	How To Navigate Through Federal Prison	39.95
	Sunny 101: The 10 Commandments Of A Boss Chick	14.95
	Total For Books	
	20% Inmate Discount -	
	Shipping/Handling +	
	Total Cost	

* Shipping/Handling 1-3 books 4.95
4-9 books 8.95
* Incarcerated individuals receive a 20% discount on each book purchase.
* Forms of Accepted Payments: Certified Checks, Institutional Checks and Money Orders.
* Bulk rates are available upon requests for orders of 10 books or more.
* Curriculum Guides are available for group sessions.
* All mail-in orders take 5-7 business days to be delivered. For prison orders, please
allow up to (3) three weeks for delivery.

SHIP TO:

Name: _____

Address: _____

_____

_____

City: _____

State: _____ Zip: _____

Made in the USA
Columbia, SC
06 November 2019